Georgia Bucket List Adventure Guide

Explore 100 Offbeat
Destinations You Must Visit!

Aaron Valdez

Canyon Press
canyon@purplelink.org

Please consider writing a review!
Just visit: purplelink.org/review

ISBN: 978-1-957590-06-6

FREE BONUS

Discover 31 Incredible Places You Can
Visit Next! Just Go To:

purplelink.org/travel

Table of Contents

Athens

Augusta

How to Use This Book

Welcome to your very own adventure guide to exploring the many wonders of the state of Georgia. Not only does this book offer the most wonderful places to visit and sights to see in the vast state, but it provides GPS coordinates for Google Maps to make exploring that much easier.

Adventure Guide
Sorted by region, this guide offers over 100 amazing wonders found in Georgia for you to see and explore. They can be visited in any order, and this book will help you keep track of where you've been and where to look forward to going next. Each section describes the area or place, what to look for, how to get there, and what you may need to bring along.

GPS Coordinates
As you can imagine, not all of the locations in this book have a physical address. Fortunately, some of our listed wonders are either located within a National Park or Reserve or near a city, town, or place of business. For those that are not associated with a specific location, it is easiest to map it using GPS coordinates.

Luckily, Google has a system of codes that converts the coordinates into pin-drop locations that Google Maps can interpret and navigate.

Each adventure in this guide includes GPS coordinates along with a physical address whenever it is available.

It is important that you are prepared for poor cell signals. It is recommended that you route your location and ensure that the directions are accessible offline. Depending on your device and the distance of some locations, you may need to travel with a backup battery source.

About Georgia

Georgia is located in the southeastern area of the United States and is full of more charm than just about any other state in the country. The state of Georgia was the last of the Confederate states to be restored to the Union on July 15, 1870. It was also the state that was at the forefront of the civil rights movement and is full of museums and history. Several nature features are must-see places in the state, including various beaches to enjoy along the coast of the Atlantic Ocean. The most popular cities to live in and visit are Atlanta, Savannah, Athens, Augusta, and Macon.

Landscape and Climate

The state of Georgia has a wide range of landscapes in various areas, each with its own beauty and charm. In the western part of the state are the lowland marsh areas that are full of rain forests, swamps, and a lot of mountains covered with snow and even glaciers. In the eastern part are more mountains in the Blue Ridge Mountain Range as well as fourteen barrier islands and coastal areas in the southeastern region. In the center of the state are plains covered with several different lakes and rivers.

Due to the large bodies of water all over the state, Georgia has a very humid climate just about everywhere you go, except for up on the tall mountains. From time to time, Georgia does experience extreme weather with the highest ever recorded temperature of 112 degrees Fahrenheit and the lowest as minus 17 degrees Fahrenheit. Several droughts have been recorded, even though the area is prone to hurricanes because it's on the coast. The worst of these hurricanes usually happen when a storm hits Florida, weakens, and travels across the land up into the state of Georgia.

Plant and Animal Life

Because of Georgia's subtropical weather, a wide variety of plant and animal life can be found in the state. There are over 250 different tree species, including 58 protected plants. From pines and oaks to sweetgum and scaly-bark, there are trees everywhere you look in this nature-filled state.

More than 90 different mammals have been found in George. There are a few different types of endangered species, such as the gray bat and the Indiana bat. More than 150 different amphibians and reptiles, such as 50 different types of salamanders, 30 different types of frogs, and 27 different turtles, reside in the water areas. Unfortunately, the swamp climate does attract many different snakes and alligators. There are also about 347 different bird species in Georgia, as well.

People and Resources

The people of the South are generally very friendly, and those that reside in Georgia are not an exception to this generalization. The state is inhabited by over 9 million people of many different ethnicities and from all over the world.

The biggest employers in the state of Georgia are in the textile industry, mostly along the I-75 corridor from Atlanta up to Chattanooga, Tennessee. Another large industry in the state is farming, as over 8 million acres of land are dedicated to farming various crops.

Other resources that make the state famous are clay production, fine marble, and abundant drinking water for the state. This area has wonderful places for swimming, fishing, and generating hydroelectric power.

Atlanta BeltLine

The Atlanta BeltLine is an older railway corridor in the heart of Georgia. Most of this area is unusable for rail, but it can be hiked. The idea behind the Atlanta BeltLine is to improve transportation for the city and add green space.

The Atlanta BeltLine connects neighborhoods and parks and is also used for art installations from time to time. Routes include the following trails: Eastside Trail, Northside Trail, Southwest Connector Trail, West End Trail, and Westside Trail.

In addition to the railway trails, there are hiking trails as well to connect the city of Atlanta even more.

Best Time to Visit: Any time of year

Pass/Permit/Fees: No known fees at this time

Closest City or Town: Atlanta, GA

Address: Atlanta BeltLine Eastside Trail, Atlanta, GA 30312

GPS Coordinates: 33.78430° N, 84.36852° W

Did You Know? The Atlanta Belt Line is projected to be completed in 2030 at an estimated cost of $4.8 billion.

Atlanta Botanical Garden

The Atlanta Botanical Garden, located in Midtown Atlanta, covers 30 acres of land, all beautifully landscaped and full of many different plants.

The botanical garden serves the community in multiple ways. Its mission statement is to "develop and maintain plant collections for the purposes of display, education, conservation, research, and enjoyment."

The garden was incorporated as a society in 1976 and is proud to host several different art exhibitions and annual art shows throughout the year. The park has a 600-ft long covered walk, known as the Kendeda Canopy Walk, that allows guests to enjoy the urban forest from up in the air.

Best Time to Visit: Any time of year

Pass/Permit/Fees: Adult: $22.95, Child (ages 3-12): $19.95, Children under 3 are free

Closest City or Town: Atlanta, GA

Address: 1345 Piedmont Ave NE, Augusta, GA 30906

GPS Coordinates: 33.79036° N, 84.37310° W

Did You Know? The average visit to the botanical gardens is 1½-2 hours to see everything the garden has to offer.

Atlanta History Center

It should come as no surprise that the city of Atlanta is bursting with history everywhere you look. The Atlanta History Center is home to 33 acres of historical houses, gardens, and other exhibitions.

This museum informs the public about the history of the area and how it came to be the city that it is today. The Atlanta History Center was created in 1926 and has many permanent and temporary exhibitions.

Best Time to Visit: Any time of year, open from Tuesday-Sunday from 9:00 a.m.-4:00 p.m., historical houses open at 11:00 a.m.

Pass/Permit/Fees: Adult: $23.41, Seniors/Student: $19.60, Youth (4-12): $9.80

Closest City or Town: Atlanta, GA

Address: 130 West Paces Ferry Rd NW, Atlanta, GA 30305

GPS Coordinates: 33.84278° N, 84.38584° W

Did You Know? Most people spend half of a day exploring at the Atlanta History Center, with a minimum of 4 hours in the museum.

Centennial Olympic Park

This 22-acre space in the middle of Atlanta is famous for hosting the 1996 Summer Olympic Games and is known as Centennial Olympic Park. The park is the reason behind the downtown revitalization and represents the billions of dollars spent to revive the city in preparation for the Olympics.

Guests are welcome to relax around the Fountain of Rings, find the commemorative brick, and enjoy playgrounds, expansive lawn areas, and gardens.

The area has several landmarks as well, all making it worth your while to visit while in Atlanta.

Best Time to Visit: Any time of year

Pass/Permit/Fees: No fee

Closest City or Town: Atlanta, GA

Address: 265 Park Ave. W NW, Atlanta, GA 30313

GPS Coordinates: 33.76192° N, 84.39435° W

Did You Know? On July 27, 1996, Eric Rudolph placed a bomb in the middle of the Centennial Olympic Park during the Olympic Games. One person was killed, and 100 were injured during this tragic and hateful bombing event.

Center for Puppetry Arts

The Center for Puppetry Arts is the largest museum for puppetry in the entire country. The core focus for the establishment is performance, education, and the on-site museum. Vincent Anthony founded the Center for Puppetry Arts in 1978.

Each year, several performances and educational programs are offered to the community. One of the most popular clinics offered by the Center for Puppetry Arts is the Create-A-Puppet Workshop, where children can build their own puppets as they learn about the art behind the craft of puppetry.

Best Time to Visit: Tuesday-Saturday from 10:00 a.m.-5:00 p.m., Sunday from noon-5:00 p.m., closed on Mondays. The last admission each day is at 4:00 p.m.

Pass/Permit/Fees: Tickets cost up to $20.

Closest City or Town: Atlanta, GA

Address: 1404 Spring St NW, Atlanta, GA 30309

GPS Coordinates: 33.79376° N, 84.38981° W

Did You Know? The Center for Puppetry Arts hosts over 600 performances each year.

Coca-Cola Roxy

The Coca-Cola Roxy, in Cumberland, Georgia, offers several performances are held each year.

The venue was built in 2017, can hold up to 4,000 guests, and has five different bars inside. The entire theater is 53,000 square feet and has two levels of seating areas.

The Coca-Cola Roxy is a destination for live music, with events held at various times throughout the year.

Best Time to Visit: Any time of year

Pass/Permit/Fees: Tickets for events vary

Closest City or Town: Atlanta

Address: 800 Battery Ave SE #500, Atlanta, GA 30339

GPS Coordinates: 33.89107° N, 84.46951° W

Did You Know? The newly renovated Roxy theater can hold 3,600 people and is located next to Truist Park in Atlanta.

Coca-Cola Space Science Center

Right along the Georgia and Alabama state line is the Coca-Cola Space Science Center. The museum is a great way to learn more about science while being entertained in the process.

This science center is home to the Challenger Learning Center mission simulator, Space Shuttle Odyssey launch simulator, and much more. Inside the Coca-Cola Space Science Center is a museum that holds various space shuttle artifacts from NASA that show how the shuttles operate. Children and adults can learn a lot from a visit to the Coca-Cola Space Science Center.

Best Time to Visit: Any time of year, open M-F from noon-4:00 p.m. and Saturday from 11:00 a.m.-5:00 p.m.

Pass/Permit/Fees: Adult: $8, Military/Seniors: $7, Children (4-10): $6, Children under 3: Free

Closest City or Town: Columbus, GA

Address: 701 Front Ave, Columbus, GA 31901

GPS Coordinates: 32.46067° N, 84.99427° W

Did You Know? The Coca-Cola Space Science Center is owned by Columbus State University.

Constitution Lakes Park

Nestled in the industrial area of Georgia is the Constitution Lakes Park, a unique and enjoyable place to visit. The park includes a wooded area trail, a lake, and the famous Dolls Head Trail.

The Dolls Head Trail is an art trail that many individuals have collaborated on to create a fun, not-commonly-known thing to do while visiting Atlanta.

Some people find this art trail to be a bit creepy, but it is fun to experience, nonetheless.

Best Time to Visit: The early morning hours are the most beautiful time as fog covers the lake.

Pass/Permit/Fees: Parking and admission are free.

Closest City or Town: Atlanta, GA

Address: 1305 S River Industrial Blvd SE, Atlanta, GA 30315

GPS Coordinates: 33.68292, 84.34414

Did You Know? The Constitution Lakes area is home to thousands of different s[species of wildlife and plant life.

David J. Sencer CDC Museum

The David J. Sencer CDC Museum is a museum for the U.S. Centers for Disease Control and Prevention and is closely affiliated with the Smithsonian Institution.

The museum works to educate visitors on how to prevent illness and disease with the use of "dynamic educational programming and engaging museum exhibitions."

The CDC Museum opened to the public in 1996 when the Olympic Games were held in Atlanta. Since 2020, the museum has been temporarily closed to the public.

Best Time to Visit: Temporarily closed

Pass/Permit/Fees: No fee

Closest City or Town: Atlanta, GA

Address: 1600 Clifton Rd, Atlanta, GA 30329

GPS Coordinates: 33.80004° N, 84.32991° W

Did You Know? This museum is temporarily closed because of Covid-19 but will hopefully be open to the public when it is safe to do so.

Fernbank Museum of Natural History

The Fernbank Museum of Natural History has many artifacts, including the skeleton of a 123-foot-long dinosaur, the largest dinosaur to ever be identified. In addition, the museum has several exhibits to show how the planet was developed.

The exhibits at the Fernbank Museum of Natural History feature several permanent and a few temporary exhibits, all designed to educate the public about natural history.

With a convenient location just outside of Atlanta, this museum is a great place to visit, right next to the historic houses and overlooking the Fernbank Forest.

Best Time to Visit: Any time of year, open daily from 10:00 a.m.-5:00 p.m.

Pass/Permit/Fees: Adult (age 13-64): $20, Senior (65+): $19, Child (3-12): $18, Under 3: Free

Closest City or Town: Atlanta, GA

Address: 767 Clifton Rd, Atlanta, GA 30307.

GPS Coordinates: 33.77481° N, 84.32752° W

Did You Know? Fernbank Museum of Natural History got its name from a nearby creek bank that is covered in ferns.

Georgia Aquarium

An aquarium is always a fun place to visit, especially if you have young children because there are a lot of interactive exhibits and hundreds of animals to observe. The Georgia Aquarium in Atlanta is one of the largest aquariums in the entire world, only behind two aquariums in China.

The Georgia Aquarium has very popular animals such as whale sharks, beluga whales, bottlenose dolphins, and manta rays. The entire aquarium contains over 11 million gallons of fresh and salt water.

Best Time to Visit: S-F from 9:00 a.m.-9:00 p.m., Sat from 8:00 a.m.-9:00 p.m.

Pass/Permit/Fees: $36.95 general admission, children under 2 are free

Closest City or Town: Atlanta, GA

Address: 225 Baker St. NW, Atlanta, GA 30313.

GPS Coordinates: 33.76369° N, 84.39457° W

Did You Know? The Georgia Aquarium is home to over 120,000 different animals, making it one of the world's largest aquariums.

Heritage Park

Heritage Park is a 364-acre park located near Atlanta that runs along the Apalachee River. This park was created to host outdoor events and to preserve the area. At the park is a 31-stall barn with an arena for showing animals, making it a great location for rodeos and stock shows.

The Heritage Park area also has mountain bike trails and a Central School House. Pack a picnic lunch and relax as you soak in the scenery all around you.

A historic cemetery and mill building are both excellent locations for taking a stroll to learn more about the history of this area.

Best Time to Visit: Any time of year

Pass/Permit/Fees: No fee

Closest City or Town: Atlanta, GA

Address: 513 Capitol Ave SE, Atlanta, GA 30312

GPS Coordinates: 33.63508° N, 84.51319° W

Did You Know? Heritage Park has the Veterans Wall of Honor and a Veterans Museum with a historic village that includes a log cabin from 1827.

High Museum of Art

The High Museum of Art was founded in 1905 as the Atlanta Art Association. In 1962, 106 Atlantans, many of them patrons of the museum, died when the plane that was supposed to bring them home from a tour of France crashed on takeoff. As a memorial, the French government sent two paintings from the Louvre, including the famous work known as "Whistler's Mother," to the Atlanta museum. The museum building was renovated in 1983 and now contains 135,000 square feet, showcasing all of the artifacts and collections in the gallery.

Best Time to Visit: Any time of year. Open Sunday noon-5:00 p.m., Closed Monday, Tuesday-Saturday 10:00 a.m.-5:00 p.m.

Pass/Permit/Fees: $16.50 per person, children under 6 are free

Closest City or Town: Atlanta, GA

Address: 1280 Peachtree St. NE, Atlanta, GA 30309

GPS Coordinates: 33.79095° N, 84.38538° W

Did You Know? The High is known for its modern architecture, designed by Richard Meier and the Renzo Piano.

Lake Lanier

Lake Lanier, named for the 19th-century Sidney Lanier, is a reservoir in northern Georgia.

It was created in 1956 when the U.S. Army Corps of Engineers built Buford Dam on the Chattahoochee River for flood control and water supply. The lake contains about 59 square miles and has over 692 miles of shoreline.

The Georgia Department of Natural Resources patrols Lake Lanier. The states of Georgia, Alabama, and Florida all have rights to the reservoir's water, and the Corps of Engineers is responsible for regulating the water flow for flood control.

Best Time to Visit: Any time of year

Pass/Permit/Fees: $2 per person, $5 for boat ramp use

Closest City or Town: Atlanta, GA

Address: 1200 Saddle Dike #3, Buford GA 30518

GPS Coordinates: 34.23259° N, 83.96149° W

Did You Know? Lake Lanier is dangerous due to tree trunks, old structures, and other debris at the bottom of the lake that can cause boats to get knocked off course.

Martin Luther King Jr. National Historic Site

Occupying about 25 acres in Atlanta, the Martin Luther King Jr. National Historic Site includes several buildings that are dedicated to memorializing the life of MLK Jr.

Included in the historic site is his boyhood home, the church where MLK Jr was baptized, and so much more. To teach more about his legacy and the life he lived, the historical site includes buildings that are all full of history and artifacts from his past.

Best Time to Visit: Open daily from 9:00 a.m.-5:00 p.m.

Pass/Permit/Fees: No fee

Closest City or Town: Atlanta, GA

Address: 450 Auburn Ave. NE, Atlanta, GA 30312.

GPS Coordinates: 33.75753° N, 84.37362° W

Did You Know? On March 25, 1965, Martin Luther King led a group of thousands on a non-violent march to the capitol steps in Montgomery, Alabama, after a 5-day walk from Selma, Alabama.

Mercedes-Benz Stadium

The Mercedes-Benz Stadium, commonly referred to as "The Benz," is located in Atlanta, and is the home stadium of the Atlanta Falcons.

The stadium hosts several events throughout the year but is mainly used as a stadium for National Football League (NFL) games. It was opened to the public on August 26, 2017, after an estimated $1.6 billion construction project.

Since the stadium is relatively new, it has hosted only a relative handful of local events and NFL games, but in 2019, Super Bowl LIII was played there.

Best Time to Visit: Open 24 hours, any day of the year

Pass/Permit/Fees: Ticket prices vary for scheduled events

Closest City or Town: Atlanta, GA

Address: 125 Ted Turner Dr. NW, Atlanta, GA 30303

GPS Coordinates: 33.76017° N, 84.39797° W

Did You Know? To run a complete marathon inside the Mercedes-Benz Stadium, runners must make 32.77 laps.

National Center for Civil and Human Rights

The National Center for Civil and Human Rights in Atlanta remembers and honors specific people who played a part in the civil rights movement. This museum was opened to the public in 2014 and has been educating and informing people about a very important time in our history since then.

The museum has several permanent exhibits. It takes guests roughly 75 minutes to see everything fully.

Best Time to Visit: Open Sunday noon-5:00 p.m., Closed Monday, Open Tuesday-Friday noon-5:00 p.m., Saturday from 10:00 a.m.-5:00 p.m.

Pass/Permit/Fees: $16 per person

Closest City or Town: Atlanta, GA

Address: 100 Ivan Allen Jr Blvd NW, Atlanta, GA 30313

GPS Coordinates: 33.76495° N, 84.39341° W

Did You Know? Human rights are acquired when born, while civil rights are obtained by being a legal member of a political state.

Ocoee River

The Ocoee River runs through the Cherokee National Forest and touches several states along its course. This 93-mile-long river flows through the Appalachian Mountains and is called the "Toccoa mile" while it is in the state of Georgia. The name "Ocoee" comes from a Cherokee name meaning "where the Catawbas lived" or "beautiful." Guests use the Ocoee River for recreational purposes, most commonly for whitewater rafting.

Best Time to Visit: June, July, and August, or any weekend during the spring or fall

Pass/Permit/Fees: Rafting prices vary, but on average, you can expect to pay anywhere from $50 to $90 for a day of whitewater rafting.

Closest City or Town: Atlanta, GA

Address: To book a rafting trip, you'll find the Rolling Thunder River Co. at 20 Hughes St, McCaysville, GA 30555.

GPS Coordinates: 35.16334° N, 84.67888° W

Did You Know? The middle part of the Ocoee River was completely dry until September of 1976.

Okefenokee Swamp

The Okefenokee Swamp in the Okefenokee National Wildlife Refuge is commonly the entry point for visitors to the refuge. The swamp contains beautiful mirror waters, islands, lakes, jungles, forests, and more. Boat tours are offered on the Indian waters, and guests can observe many different types of wildlife. Okefenokee Swamp Park has several highlights, such as the low-water boardwalk, an observation tower 90 feet off of the ground, the "Eye on Nature Wildlife Show," and more.

Best Time to Visit: Fall months as the weather and crowds are ideal

Pass/Permit/Fees: Adults (ages 12 and up): $20, Children (ages 3-11): $19, Children (under 2): Free

Closest City or Town: Atlanta, GA

Address: The Okefenokee Swamp Park is at 5700 Okefenokee Swamp Park Rd, Waycross, GA 31503, and the Okefenokee National Wildlife Refuge is found at 2700 Suwannee Canal Road, Folkston, GA 31537.

GPS Coordinates: 30.66984° N, 82.33300° W

Did You Know? The Okefenokee Swamp is the largest blackwater swamp in the country and a habitat for the bald eagle and American alligator.

Piedmont Park

Piedmont Park in the heart of Atlanta is a very popular urban park in the area. When it was originally crafted and designed, the purpose was to host several expositions, which it did in 1887 and 1895.

Throughout the years, Piedmont Park has continued to be a core location for athletics in the city. The Atlanta Crackers, the city's first professional baseball team, played here in 1904.

In addition to these historic events, the park has tennis courts, picnic areas, a dock, a visitor center, and two playgrounds.

Best Time to Visit: Open daily from dusk until dawn

Pass/Permit/Fees: No fee

Closest City or Town: Atlanta, GA

Address: 1320 Monroe Dr. NE, Atlanta, GA 30306

GPS Coordinates: 33.78857° N, 84.37285° W

Did You Know? Piedmont Park has a lot of walking and running paths across the area with picnic tables, grilles, and water fountains scattered throughout for the convenience of visitors.

Pine Mountain Trail

The Pine Mountain Trail is made up of seven different loops that many people enjoy taking slowly. Each one can be a full-day trip.

The most popular, Pine Mountain Trail, is 23 miles long. It's located near Cartersville, Georgia. Here, hikers and visitors can see several different wildflowers and wildlife.

The trail is accessible at any time during the year, and guests are welcome to bring their pets, as long as they are kept on a leash and cleaned up after.

Best Time to Visit: Any time of year

Pass/Permit/Fees: $5 per day per vehicle. $50 for a year pass

Closest City or Town: Atlanta, GA

Address: The Pine Mountain Trailhead is found at Komatsu Dr. SE, Cartersville, GA 30121.

GPS Coordinates: 34.28315° N, 85.06419° W

Did You Know? The Pine Mountain Trail is a great habitat for bears, so you should always be careful when hiking through bear country.

Ponce City Market

The Ponce City Market, in the Ponce de Leon Avenue area, is a community with a number of different buildings. The purpose is "to move Atlanta forward while maintaining and emphasizing the city's unique history and culture."

Commonly called "PCM" by locals, the market includes restaurants, places to live, an amusement park on the roof, retail locations, and much more. In addition to all of the fun things the area has to offer, there is a lot of rich history here as well.

In 1925, Ponce City Market was built and used as a Sears store, which closed in 1989. It covers 2.1 million square feet of space and is nine stories high.

Best Time to Visit: Any time of year

Pass/Permit/Fees: No fee

Closest City or Town: Atlanta, GA

Address: 675 Ponce de Leon Ave. NE, Atlanta, GA, 30308.

GPS Coordinates: 33.77379° N, 84.36405° W

Did You Know? Ponce City Market is named after Ponce de Leon, an explorer who was searching for the Fountain of Youth.

SkyView Atlanta

Some parts of the city are designed with the sole purpose of entertainment and fun; SkyView Atlanta is one of those places. It features a 20-story Ferris wheel in the middle of Centennial Park that allows guests to see the entire city from a climate-controlled gondola.

If you are interested in the more expensive tickets, SkyView Atlanta allows guests and riders to see the entire city from a Ferrari-style seat with a glass-floored gondola.

Best Time to Visit: Open Monday-Thursday from noon-10pm, Friday from noon-midnight, Saturday from 10:00 a.m.-midnight, and Sunday from 10:00 a.m.-10:00 p.m.

Pass/Permit/Fees: Adult: $14.75, Children (ages 3-11): $9.75, Children under 2 are free

Closest City or Town: Atlanta, GA

Address: 168 Luckie St. NW, Atlanta, GA 30303.

GPS Coordinates: 33.75965° N, 84.39057° W

Did You Know? The entire ride on SkyView Atlanta lasts between 7 and 12 minutes.

SunTrust/Truist Park

SunTrust Park, which became Truist Park in 2020, is the home stadium for the Atlanta Braves.

Built at a cost of $622 million, the park opened for the 2017 season. It offers concessions, gift shops, and an enjoyable baseball experience for adults and children.

The original naming rights were bought by SunTrust Bank on a 25-year deal. When SunTrust merged with . in January 2020 to become Truist Financial, the name changed accordingly.

Best Time to Visit: Any time during baseball season

Pass/Permit/Fees: Ticket prices depend on seat location and the teams playing.

Closest City or Town: Atlanta, GA

Address: 755 Battery Ave. SE, Atlanta GA, 30339.

GPS Coordinates: 33.89213° N, 84.46853° W

Did You Know? Although the number changes from time to time, there are over 23 restaurant and distillery options available at SunTrust/Truist Park!

The Fox Theatre

The Fox Theatre originally opened as a movie palace in 1929 with a 3600-pipe organ to accompany the ballet, movie, or other events performed in this theatre.

Modern-day performances most commonly include touring Broadway shows, concerts, comedy performances, ballet, tours, and more.

For people that are interested in learning more about the Fox Theatre, a one-hour guided tour allows guests to take a closer look at its history and inner workings.

Best Time to Visit: Any time of year

Pass/Permit/Fees: Ticket costs depend on the show being performed

Closest City or Town: Atlanta, GA

Address: 660 Peachtree St. NE, Atlanta, GA 30308.

GPS Coordinates: 33.77334° N, 84.38436° W

Did You Know? The Fox Theatre has 4,665 seats and usually holds up to 150 different performances each year!

Zoo Atlanta

Visiting a zoo is always fun, no matter where you are from or who you are with. Taking in the landscaping and observing the animals is something that everyone can enjoy, especially at the Zoo Atlanta.

Established in 1886, Zoo Atlanta is located in Grant Park. In 1889, a traveling menagerie came through Atlanta, and the exotic animals remained as the first major donation to the zoo.

The zoo was reformed in 2000 and made it into the top 10 zoos to visit, after formerly being in the list of the top ten worst zoos in the country. Zoo Atlanta offers educational programs, seasonal events, and so much more.

Best Time to Visit: Open daily from 9:00 a.m.-3:30 pm

Pass/Permit/Fees: Adult: $29.99, Child: $21.99, under 2: Free

Closest City or Town: Atlanta, GA

Address: 800 Cherokee Ave. SE, Atlanta, GA 30315.

GPS Coordinates: 33.73450° N, 84.37204° W

Did You Know? The Zoo Atlanta is home to over 1,500 animals from over 220 species.

Downtown Athens

Downtown Athens is the oldest part of the city, showcasing restored buildings from the Victorian period that are all full of creativity. While visiting Downtown Athens, guests can expect to see many different restaurants, shops, and live music venues.

Among several must-see items here, the Morton Theatre is one of the oldest vaudeville theaters in the country. Stop for a lunch or enjoy the nightlife here because there is so much to offer in Downtown Athens, Georgia.

Best Time to Visit: Any time of year

Pass/Permit/Fees: No fee

Closest City or Town: Athens, GA

Address: 125 W Washington St Suite 121, Athens, GA 30601

GPS Coordinates: 33.95696° N, 83.37844° W

Did You Know? The Downtown Athens area is about 70 miles long, with so much to explore and enjoy!

Sandy Creek Nature Center

The Sandy Creek Nature Center is a 225-acre outdoor area for exploration, education, and enjoyment. This area contains more than 4 miles of hiking trails and opportunities to explore wetlands and woodlands.

The visitors center has live animals, aquariums, history exhibits, a resource library, and much more, all in an environmentally friendly building. On site is a log house built in 1815 for guests to explore in addition to all of the other things offered in the visitor center and Sandy Creek Nature Center.

Best Time to Visit: Closed Sunday-Monday, Open Tuesday-Saturday from 8:30 a.m.-5:30 p.m.

Pass/Permit/Fees: No fee

Closest City or Town: Athens, GA

Address: 205 Old Commerce Rd, Athens, GA 30607.

GPS Coordinates: 33.98675° N, 83.38227° W

Did You Know? The Sandy Creek Nature Center is a terrific way to escape the busy everyday activities and relax and enjoy the outdoors.

State Botanical Garden of Georgia

The State Botanical Garden of Georgia in Athens, Georgia, covers 313 acres. The botanical garden is beautiful to visit and offers guests a wide variety of plants and flowers to observe and enjoy.

There are 11 different botanical/horticultural groupings at the State Botanical Garden of Georgia, each offering different flowers and organized landscaping to soak in.

The gardens have over 5 miles of hiking and nature trails, so hitting your step goal will not be a problem here!

Best Time to Visit: Open daily from 8:00 a.m.-7:00 p.m.

Pass/Permit/Fees: No fee

Closest City or Town: Athens, GA

Address: 2450 S Milledge Ave, Athens, GA 30605.

GPS Coordinates: 33.90206° N, 83.38537° W

Did You Know? The State Botanical Garden of Georgia has been marked as a major area for birding by the Georgia Audubon Society, meaning it is an excellent place to find a variety of birds!

Terrapin Brewery

The Terrapin Brewery, or Terrapin Beer Co., in Athens, GA, was created by Brian "Spike" Buckowski and John Cochran. The building Terrapin Brewery is located in contains 40,000 square feet, and it is said to offer the best beer in the Southeast.

There are tours and beer tastings for guests, but you are required to wear closed-toe shoes, safety glasses, and ear protection. The safety glasses and earplugs are provided by Terrapin Beer Co. The brewery is powered by solar energy to keep its craft eco-friendly. This venue often hosts live music. Dogs and children are welcome to join their parents. Games and space are available for socializing outside.

Best Time to Visit: For event and tour information, contact the brewery directly.

Pass/Permit/Fees: No fee, unless you take a guided tour and purchase a drink

Closest City or Town: Athens, GA

Address: 265 Newton Bridge Rd, Athens, GA 30607.

GPS Coordinates: 33.98104° N, 83.39627° W

Did You Know? Terrapin employs more female brewers than any other craft-size brewery in the U.S.

The Athens Double-Barreled Cannon

The Athens Double-Barreled Cannon, located in Athens, interestingly has never been used. The cannon was created as an experiment, something that had never been done before, making it a unique artifact from the Civil War period.

The idea behind this cannon was to load two balls connected by a chain. When the cannon was fired, the chain would come out of the cannon and cut down any soldiers in the path of this missile. Unfortunately, when the cannon was fired in testing rounds, the cannonballs were uncontrollable, so it couldn't be used in warfare.

Best Time to Visit: Open 24 hours

Pass/Permit/Fees: No fee

Closest City or Town: Athens, GA

Address: 301 College Ave, Athens, GA 30601.

GPS Coordinates: 33.96076° N, 83.37439° W

Did You Know? The unsuccessful Athens Double-Barreled Cannon was created by John Gilleland in 1862 but was never used in warfare because it was not a successful design.

Augusta Canal

The Augusta Canal is a great place to explore via foot, bike, or boat on a guided boat tour through the area. There are several areas to hike or ride your bike to soak in the history and scenery as you explore the canal area.

The Augusta Canal is a location where guests can discover the country's only industrial power canal that is still being used for the original intended purpose.

Whether you prefer to hike the trails or take the boat tour, there is a lot to learn at the Augusta Canal.

Best Time to Visit: Any time of year

Pass/Permit/Fees: Free with boat tour or Adult: $6, Senior/Student/Military: $4

Closest City or Town: Augusta, GA

Address: 2421 Riverlook Dr., Augusta, GA 30904

GPS Coordinates: 33.53168° N, 82.02345° W

Did You Know? The Augusta Canal was originally built in 1845 as a power, water, and transportation source for the American South.

Augusta Downtown Historic District

The Augusta Downtown Historic District is the historic commercial area off Broad Street, along the Savannah River and the railroad track. Guests can explore how the city was laid out in the 1700 and 1800s.

The district has many buildings that are significant for their architectural styles from 1801 to 1967. As Georgia's second oldest city, there are a lot of historical things to discover and learn more about in Augusta, GA.

Best Time to Visit: Any time of year

Pass/Permit/Fees: No fee

Closest City or Town: Augusta, GA

Address: The Augusta Downtown Historic District is located between 4th and 13th Streets and is accessed via Broad St.

GPS Coordinates: 33.46839° N, 81.95303° W

Did You Know? Some people might be familiar with the town of Augusta because of the annual Masters' Golf Tournament that is held in the first full week of April every year.

Augusta Museum of History

The Augusta Museum of History in Augusta, GA, is home to many artifacts from the area's history. The museum was founded in 1937 and includes artifacts from James Brown, the Godfather of Soul.

There are artifacts from slave-made pottery, an 1869 steam fire engine that was destroyed and damaged in a fire, and much more at the Augusta Museum of History.

This museum is the only museum in the Central Savannah River Area, so it is full of history and offers much to learn.

Best Time to Visit: Any time of year, Sunday 1:00 p.m.- 5:00 p.m., Thursday-Saturday 10:00 a.m.-5:00 p.m.

Pass/Permit/Fees: Adults: $5, Seniors: $4, Children (6-18): $3, Under 6: Free

Closest City or Town: Augusta, GA

Address: 560 Reynolds St., Augusta, GA 30901

GPS Coordinates: 33.47501° N, 81.95879° W

Did You Know? The Augusta Museum of History is the oldest museum that works to preserve the past and all of the artifacts from the previous periods.

Forest Hills Golf Club

The Forest Hills Golf Club in Augusta, Georgia, is owned by the nearby Augusta University. The 18-hole course was designed by Donald Ross in 1926 and was renovated in 2003 by the Arnold Palmer Company.

This golf course has hosted several famous events and tournaments, including the 1930 Southeastern Open and, more recently, the 3M Augusta Invitational.

Best Time to Visit: Open daily from 7:00 a.m.-6:00 p.m.

Pass/Permit/Fees: 18 holes (Walking): M-Th ($29), Friday-Sunday ($39)
18 holes (Cart Included): M-Th ($49), Friday-Sunday ($59),
9 holes (Cart Included): M-Th ($30), Friday-Sunday ($37)

Closest City or Town: Augusta, GA

Address: 1500 Comfort Rd, Augusta, GA 30909.

GPS Coordinates: 33.47355° N, 82.04733° W

Did You Know? The Forest Hills Golf Club has a practice area, restaurant, and banquet facility in addition to the golf course.

James Brown Statue

James Brown, the Godfather of Soul and the "hardest working man in show business," was honored with this statue in Augusta, Georgia, to celebrate his legacy and contribution to music.

The statue was created by an orthopedic surgeon named John Savage. It makes James Brown appear larger and taller than he was in real life. Ironically, the statue is situated so that Brown has his back toward Georgia and his face looking toward South Carolina, and it is in a very difficult place to visit.

Best Time to Visit: Any time of year; just be careful because the statue is located in the middle of a busy intersection.

Pass/Permit/Fees: No fee

Closest City or Town: Augusta, GA

Address: 830 Broad St., Augusta, GA 30901

GPS Coordinates: 33.47669° N, 81.96642° W

Did You Know? Many people have wanted to relocate this statue to a more beautiful location that is easier to visit, but it has not been done yet, so he remains in the original location in the hot Georgia sun.

Lucy Craft Laney Museum of Black History

The Lucy Craft Laney Museum of Black History is the largest African American museum in the Augusta area. In 1991, the museum was opened to the public to honor Lucy Craft Laney in the house where she used to live.

The mission of this museum is to preserve the history and artifacts of the time and especially to encourage guests to learn more about the legacy of Lucy Craft Laney. With the use of exhibits and programs throughout the year, the museum educates the public and accomplishes its mission.

Best Time to Visit: Closed Sundays, Open Monday-Saturday from 9:00 a.m.-5:00 p.m.

Pass/Permit/Fees: $7 Adults, $3 Children 18 and under, $5 seniors

Closest City or Town: Augusta, GA

Address: 1116 Phillips St, Augusta, GA 30901.

GPS Coordinates: 33.46742° N, 81.98143° W

Did You Know? Lucy Craft Laney was an educator who founded Augusta's first school for black children in 1883 and was the first African American to be honored with a portrait in the Georgia state capital.

Meadow Garden

The Meadow Garden is an 18th-century home that has been turned into a museum to remember the life of George Walton, a politician from Augusta, Georgia. Walton was one of the three Georgians who signed the Declaration of Independence. He also served as the state's governor and U.S. senator.

The museum at the Meadow Garden was declared a National Historic Landmark in 1981. There is a cottage feel to the home. The front of the house has columns that were added by the Daughters of the American Revolution to give it a better appearance from the curb.

Best Time to Visit: Open Monday-Friday 10:00 a.m.-4:00 p.m.

Pass/Permit/Fees: Adults: $4, Children: $1

Closest City or Town: Augusta, GA

Address: 1320 Independence Dr., Augusta, GA 30901.

GPS Coordinates: 33.47462° N, 81.97899° W

Did You Know? The Georgia State Society and the Daughters of the American Revolution have owned the Meadow Garden home since 1901.

Phinizy Swamp Nature Park

The Phinizy Swamp Nature Park in Augusta, Georgia, covers 1,100 acres of wet and woodlands. There are many different aspects of nature to observe and soak in.

Another reason people love to visit the Phinizy Swamp Nature Park is to see all of the wildlife, as well. The area features diverse and interesting species of birds, in addition to reptiles like frogs and snakes.

Due to the large quantity of dangerous and poisonous snakes, hunting and fishing are not allowed.

Best Time to Visit: Any time of year, open daily from 7:00 a.m.-6:00 p.m.

Pass/Permit/Fees: No fee

Closest City or Town: Augusta, GA

Address: 1858 Lock and Dam Rd, Augusta, GA 30906.

GPS Coordinates: 33.38438° N, 81.96589° W

Did You Know? There are alligator habitats at the Phinizy Swamp Nature Park, so you should always proceed with caution when visiting the area because these are very dangerous creatures.

Sacred Heart Cultural Center

The Sacred Heart Cultural Center, also called the Sacred Heart Catholic Church, hosts events for the Catholic Church in Augusta, Georgia. This beautiful building stands out as a landmark for the entire city of Augusta.

This church offered its first service in 1900. In 1972, the building was listed on the National Register of Historic Places and was renovated in 1987 by the Knox Foundation.

The Sacred Heart Cultural Center has events throughout the year, such as wine festivals, choir concerts, holiday events, and a garden festival.

Best Time to Visit: Open Monday-Friday 9:00 a.m.-5:00 p.m. Closed Saturday and Sundays.

Pass/Permit/Fees: No fee

Closest City or Town: Augusta, GA

Address: 1301 Greene St, Augusta, GA 30901.

GPS Coordinates: 33.47767° N, 81.97477° W

Did You Know? This church is said to be the best example of Victorian masonry work in Georgia and boasts beautiful architecture everywhere you look.

Woodrow Wilson Boyhood Home

This historical landmark, Woodrow Wilson's Boyhood Home, is open to the public for guided tours by appointment only. It's a museum that shows the early life of President Wilson and what it was like for him to grow up during the Civil War and Reconstruction.

The museum is both educational and enjoyable for guests as they discover the rich history involved with our 28th president. In addition to regularly scheduled tours, there are also holiday tours offered, depending on what time of year you visit.

Best Time to Visit: Any time of year

Pass/Permit/Fees: $5 for adults, $4 for seniors, $3 for students k-12

Closest City or Town: Augusta, GA

Address: 419 7th St., Augusta, GA 30901

GPS Coordinates: 33.47254° N, 81.96456° W

Did You Know? Woodrow Wilson is famous partially for being the first president to appoint a Jewish justice to the Supreme Court.

Lake Seminole

Lake Seminole, in the southwest corner of the state, is maintained by the U.S. Army Corps of Engineers. The lake covers 37,500 acres of land and has 376 miles of shoreline.

People often visit this lake to fish, boat, and enjoy the outdoors. The various kinds of fish found in Lake Seminole include largemouth bass, catfish, striped bass, and crappie, as well as alligators and snakes.

The smaller ponds around the lake also have large alligators, so if you plan to visit this area, always be careful!

Best Time to Visit: The best time to visit is between January and May for largemouth bass fishing.

Pass/Permit/Fees: No fee

Closest City or Town: Bainbridge, GA

Address: 7863 Reynolds Landing Rd, Donalsonville, GA 39845

GPS Coordinates: 30.78566° N, 84.82393° W

Did You Know? Lake Seminole is a reservoir that was created when the U.S. Army Corps of Engineers built the Jim Woodruff Lock and Dam in 1952.

Lower Conasauga River Trail

The Lower Conasauga River Trail begins at Betty Gap and travels through the green forest and creeks. The forest is home to very wide-trunked trees and bright green ferns and moss growing all over the trail.

After 1.3 miles, the trail meets the first of 18 river crossings, and the rocks are very slippery in this area. The best way to get through is to walk or swim very carefully to avoid injury. Throughout the trail, hikers will travel through different elevations and terrains.

Best Time to Visit: Not during times of rainfall, and it is suggested that you wait one week after a rainfall to make sure the river is low and the rocks are not slippery.

Pass/Permit/Fees: No fee

Closest City or Town: Beaverdale, GA

Address: The Lower Conasauga River Trail is found in the Cohutta Wilderness and starts at Betty Gap, located at USFS 64, Ellijay, GA 30540. These are remote, extensive trail systems. Please pack and plan accordingly.

GPS Coordinates: 34.96682° N, 84.65164° W

Did You Know? The Lower Conasauga River Trail covers 15 miles of land, is accessible year-round, and is dog-friendly.

Blood Mountain Loop

The Blood Mountain Loop is one of the most visited hiking locations in the state. It stands high over the surrounding mountains, making it the highest spot on the Appalachian Trail in Georgia.

A hike that goes all the way around the mountain begins at Neels Gap on the Byron Reece Trail. On this trek, you will travel through steam valleys, forest canopies, and Flat Rock Gap.

The entire trip is 13 miles long and is a great option if you love to backpack.

Best Time to Visit: Any time of year

Pass/Permit/Fees: Several groups offer a day hike option and ask for a $15 donation to their organization. If you hike alone, there is no cost.

Closest City or Town: Blairsville, GA

Address: Byron Reece Memorial Trail, Blairsville, GA 30512.

GPS Coordinates: 34.72377° N, -83.95363° W

Did You Know? This hike is considered difficult, and there are not many campsites, so make sure you bring what you will need if you plan to hike the entire loop.

Jekyll Island

Jekyll Island is part of the Golden Isles, owned by the state of Georgia. This island was historically used by the natural owners of the area and was evacuated during World War II. The island is now a very popular tourist destination, and guided tours of the historical sites are available.

Best Time to Visit: September, October, and November are the best times to visit.

Pass/Permit/Fees: Bicycles and pedestrians enter at no charge. Automobile charges are $8 per day or $55 for an annual parking pass. For oversized vehicles, the cost is $12 per day and $100 per year.

Closest City or Town: Brunswick, GA

Address: The Jekyll Island Guest Information Center is located at 901 Downing Musgrove Causeway Jekyll Island, GA 31527.

GPS Coordinates: 31.07890° N, 81.40794° W

Did You Know? Jekyll Island has been a vacation destination for over 3,500 years!

St. Simons Island

St. Simons Island, the largest of the barrier islands off the coast of Georgia, was made famous by the writing of poet Sidney Lanier. This island is a great family destination because of the number of attractions and things to do. St. Simons Island offers museums, golf courses, beaches, and shops and also hosts several events throughout the year. From kayaking to fishing and biking, the island has something for everyone. If you enjoy trying new restaurants, then this island is for you!

Best Time to Visit: The best time to visit the island is in March and April, when the weather is ideal.

Pass/Permit/Fees: $8 per standard car per day, $55 for an annual pass. For oversized vehicles, the cost is $12 per car per day and $100 for an annual pass.

Closest City or Town: Brunswick, GA

Address: There are many places to visit on St. Simons Island, but a good place to start is Fort Frederica National Monument at 6515 Frederica Rd, St Simons Island, GA 31522.

GPS Coordinates: 31.18049° N, 81.38669° W

Did You Know? The island has amazing history, including a lighthouse built in 1872. the St. Simons Lighthouse Museum is close by for guests to explore.

Cochran Mill Park

Cochran Mill Park, about 20 miles southwest of the Atlanta Airport, is a great destination for observing the beauty of nature. The park has amazing waterfalls, big boulders, rock outcrops, native azaleas, mountains, and the ruins of three historic mills.

Included at Cochran Mill Park are 18 miles of different trails, 2.5 Interpretive Trail, an information desk, horseback riding options, mountain bike trails, and running opportunities.

Best Time to Visit: Not after recent rainstorms because the trails can get muddy and very slippery. Park is open from 30 minutes before sunrise until 30 minutes after sunset.

Pass/Permit/Fees: $5 parking fee

Closest City or Town: Chattahoochee Hills, GA

Address: 5201-6399 Cochran Mill Rd, Chattahoochee Hills, GA 30268.

GPS Coordinates: 33.57243° N, 84.71492° W

Did You Know? Cochran Mill Park is a dog-friendly park, but always be sure to clean up after your pet to keep the area beautiful for all guests.

Stone Mountain

Stone Mountain Park is in the middle of 3,200 acres of nature and is full of fun activities for the entire family. This park offers outdoor recreational things to do as well as on-site places to stay.

Some of the things to do include a summit skyride, dinosaur exploration area, outdoor miniature golf, historical houses and antiques, scenic railroad, a museum, amusement park rides, and so much more.

The entire area is on top of a giant piece of granite that creates the surface of the mountain. A 1-mile hike that takes guests to the summit of the mountain if you are unable to take the sky ride.

Best Time to Visit: March 19 until June 3 is ideal.

Pass/Permit/Fees: Adults (ages 12+): $59.95, Children (ages 3+): $31.95

Closest City or Town: Clarkston, GA

Address: 1000 Robert E Lee Blvd., GA 30087

GPS Coordinates: 33.81321° N, 84.16975° W

Did You Know? The granite piece that makes up stone mountain weighs over 1 trillion pounds and covers over 583 acres of land.

DeSoto Falls

DeSoto Falls are located along the DeSoto Falls Trail in the area where armor was found from DeSoto's expedition in the 1500s. The hike is a 2-mile adventure with a forest full of creeks and breathtaking waterfalls. This hike is considered kid-friendly, with moderate elevation changes as you make your journey.

A viewing platform for the DeSoto Falls allows you to relax and soak in the beauty of the waterfall. The trail does have slippery rocks, so always proceed with caution as the fast-moving water can be dangerous. This waterfall is not safe for climbing, swimming, or jumping.

Best Time to Visit: Any time of year

Pass/Permit/Fees: $4 per vehicle at the park entrance.

Closest City or Town: Cleveland, GA

Address: 18365 U.S.-129, Cleveland, GA 30528

GPS Coordinates: 34.71971° N, 83.91883° W

Did You Know? The DeSoto Falls Trail is heavily used by hikers of all different skill levels. Dogs are welcome as long as you clean up after them.

Helen

Helen, Georgia, is a small town with a population of only 430 people but one of the most visited locations in the entire state. This tiny town is full of charm and festivals, especially their annual Oktoberfest.

Around the town of Helen are several outdoor activities, such as visiting the Anna Ruby Falls, Unicoi State Park, Habersham Vineyards and Winery, and so much more.

The tiny but mighty town of Helen has something for everyone and is a great family vacation destination.

Best Time to Visit: Any time of year

Pass/Permit/Fees: No fee

Closest City or Town: Cleveland, GA

Address: 726 Brucken Strasse, Helen, GA 30545

GPS Coordinates: 34.70257° N, 83.72426° W

Did You Know? Helen has a very special history and has adopted a "classic south-German style" that is evident everywhere you look in the city.

Yonah Mountain Trail

The Yonah Mountain Trail is a moderately rated hike but well worth every second for the views when you reach the summit. This is a very popular hike that climbs up Yonah Mountain to overlook the southern Appalachian Mountain range. There are several asymmetrical areas with exposed rock outcroppings that make the area desirable for hikers and rock climbers.

While the views are breathtaking, there are sheer cliff edges that are very dangerous without the proper hiking gear. Always stay away from the edge, and be sure to carefully place each step you take.

Best Time to Visit: Between February and November

Pass/Permit/Fees: No fee

Closest City or Town: Cleveland, GA

Address: GA-75, Cleveland, GA 30528

GPS Coordinates: 34.64112° N, 83.72501° W

Did You Know? The name "Yonah" is the Cherokee word for "bear," so proceed with caution!

Columbus Museum

Founded in 1953, the Columbus Museum is full of American art history and many artifacts. Guests can view the permanent collections as well as exhibitions that are changed periodically.

The Columbus Museum brings together various art artifacts from America as well as regional pieces from the Chattahoochee Valley.

Several events and programs are held throughout the year, as well as a virtual museum, gift shop, and plenty of things to discover and learn more about.

Best Time to Visit: Open from Tuesday-Saturday from 10:00 a.m.-5:00 p.m., Sunday from 1:00 p.m.-5:00 p.m., and closed on Mondays.

Pass/Permit/Fees: Adult: $14, Children: $5

Closest City or Town: Columbus, GA

Address: 1251 Wynnton Rd, Columbus, GA 31906

GPS Coordinates: 32.46766° N, 84.97158° W

Did You Know? The Columbus Museum was chartered in 1941 and opened to the public in 1953.

MidTown Columbus

MidTown Columbus is a six-mile area in Columbus, Georgia, that has many neighborhoods, schools, historical areas, parks, and green spaces. There are also several museums, a library, an aquatic center, and the international headquarters for Aflac.

About 22,000 people live in the 6-mile area of MidTown Columbus. When out exploring the MidTown area, guests are likely to see multiple cyclists because there is a new Fall Line Trace bike trail as well as quick access to the 14-mile Riverwalk. Locals and guests enjoy walking through parks and trails in the area because it is a very friendly and welcoming place.

Best Time to Visit: Any time of year

Pass/Permit/Fees: No fee

Closest City or Town: Columbus, GA

Address: 3201 Macon Rd, Columbus, GA 31906. This parking garage is a seven-minute walk from MidTown.

GPS Coordinates: 32.47920° N, 84.94398° W

Did You Know? MidTown Columbus is a river city that was founded in 1828. It is a famous site from the Civil War with a few historical locations for guests to visit.

National Civil War Naval Museum

The National Civil War Naval Museum is a 40,000 square foot building that houses the remains of two Confederate States Navy vessels. Here at the museum are several weapons, equipment, and uniforms from the U.S. Navy and the Confederate States Navy.

The National Civil War Naval Museum is one of the only museums in the country that tells both sides of the events of the Civil War.

First opened in 1962, this museum has been educating the public for many years. It changed locations in 2001.

Best Time to Visit: Open Sunday 12:30-4:30pm, Monday-Saturday from 10:00 a.m.-4:30pm

Pass/Permit/Fees: $7 per person

Closest City or Town: Columbus, GA

Address: 1002 Victory Dr., Columbus, GA 31901.

GPS Coordinates: 32.44776° N, 84.97725° W

Did You Know? The National Civil War Naval Museum overlooks the Chattahoochee River.

National Infantry Museum and Soldier Center

The National Infantry Museum and Soldier Center in Columbus, Georgia, contains 190,000 square feet.

This museum shows the chronological history of the U.S. Army infantryman from the time of the American Revolution until modern times and the war in Afghanistan.

At this museum, guests will learn the values of the soldier, including loyalty, duty, respect, selfless service, honor, integrity, and personal courage.

Best Time to Visit: Open Sunday from 11:00 a.m.-5:00 p.m., Saturday from 9:00 a.m.-5:00 p.m.

Pass/Permit/Fees: No fee, donations welcomed

Closest City or Town: Columbus, GA

Address: 1775 Legacy Way, Columbus, GA, 31903.

GPS Coordinates: 32.38933° N, 84.95357° W

Did You Know? The National Infantry Museum and Soldier Center has the most artifacts from military use in the entire world.

Oxbow Meadows Environmental Learning Center

The Oxbow Meadows Environmental Learning Center, near the Chattahoochee River, allows guests to soak up the beauty of the area and learn more about nature. The learning center has two trails for hikers or walkers and promises sightings of birds, turtles, dragonflies, and butterflies.

At this learning center, some activities allow children and adults to experience things firsthand in the area. Displays feature several different mammals, birds, and other animals that are native to the area.

Best Time to Visit: Closed Sunday and Monday, open from Tuesday-Saturday from 9:00 a.m.-4:00 p.m.

Pass/Permit/Fees: No fee

Closest City or Town: Columbus, GA

Address: 3535 S Lumpkin Rd, Columbus, GA, 31903.

GPS Coordinates: 32.38694° N, 84.95878° W

Did You Know? This learning center was opened in1995 as a group effort with the Columbus State University.

RiverCenter for the Performing Arts

The RiverCenter for the Performing Arts is a performance hall in Columbus, Georgia, that has a modern feel. The purpose of the performance hall is to enrich the Chattahoochee Valley region through the arts.

This is a 245,000square-foot building that blends the past with the present in its architectural and decorative choices. The RiverCenter for the Performing Arts concert venue seats 2,000 people and is the home stage for the Columbus Symphony Orchestra. There are several performance areas in the facility, one of which seats 430 people.

Best Time to Visit: Any time of year

Pass/Permit/Fees: Ticket prices depend on the performance

Closest City or Town: Columbus, GA

Address: 900 Broadway, Columbus, GA, 31901.

GPS Coordinates: 32.46456° N, 84.99047° W

Did You Know? The RiverCenter for the Performing Arts is used for musical concerts, dance performances, conferences, and lectures.

Springer Opera House

In the historic downtown area of Columbus, Georgia, is the Springer Opera House, a historic theatre that opened in 1871. This theater was named the state theater by Governor Jimmy Carter for the 1971-72 season and has had several famous performers come through for concerts.

The architecture is period-original and dates to 1871, the very first year the city existed. Visiting the theater for a performance is recommended but, if you are just traveling on a non-show day, it is worth it to stop by and check out the beauty of the theater.

Best Time to Visit: Tuesday-Friday from 9:00 a.m.-5:00 p.m.

Pass/Permit/Fees: Ticket costs depend on the play or performance taking place

Closest City or Town: Columbus, GA

Address: 103 E 10th St, Columbus, GA 31901.

GPS Coordinates: 32.46550° N, 84.98981° W

Did You Know? When the Springer Opera House was originally built, it was the best and nicest theater between New York City and New Orleans.

Lake Blackshear

Lake Blackshear is a man-made lake that is full of opportunities to boat, fish, and waterski. The lake was built along the Flint River and named after General David Blackshear, who fought in the American Revolution and the War of 1812.

Lake Blackshear is 20 miles long and is rarely more than a mile wide at the widest point. It offers beautiful views to guests as well as many outdoor recreational opportunities.

Swimming is allowed because only one alligator was found several years ago, but it was not in the lake itself; it was found in a nearby ditch.

Best Time to Visit: Any time of year

Pass/Permit/Fees: No fee

Closest City or Town: Cordele, GA

Address: 2459 U.S. 280, Cordele, GA 31015

GPS Coordinates: 31.96115° N, 83.92765° W

Did You Know? Lake Blackshear was created by the construction of the Crisp Count Power Dam from 1925 to 1930.

Grassy Mountain Tower Trail

The views from the Grassy Mountain Tower Trail are said to be among the best in Georgia. The hike begins at the Lake Conasauga picnic area. When you reach the lake on the hike, the trail turns right and will follow the lake counterclockwise. Along the trail, you will see many different wooded bridges and boardwalks along the shore of the lake. After 2.6 miles of hiking, you will reach the trail's summit and end up at the Grassy Mountain fire tower, which overlooks the tree line. When you climb up the steps of the tower, you will have a beautiful 360-degree view of the Cohutta Wilderness and Fort Mountain. This area is very remote, and it is recommended that guests tell someone where they are going and keep a GPS compass on them at all times in the event of getting lost.

Best Time to Visit: Avoid times with heavy rainfall

Pass/Permit/Fees: No fee

Closest City or Town: Crandall, GA

Address: There is not a specific address, but the trail begins at the Lake Conasauga Picnic and Swim Site, Tibbs Trail, Chatsworth, GA 30705.

GPS Coordinates: 34.86701° N, 84.67090° W

Did You Know? The entire trail is about 4 miles long and is very remote, so always proceed with caution.

Dahlonega Gold Museum

The Dahlonega Gold Museum was created to allow visitors to take a closer look at the state of Georgia and the history of the area.

About 20 years before the California Gold Rush, thousands of people traveled to Georgia, where the nation's very first gold rush happened.

The museum was restored by the state of Georgia and is one of the most visited locations in the entire state. It includes a 23-minute video explaining the mining techniques and more from the gold rush days.

Best Time to Visit: Open M-Sat from 9:00 a.m.-4:45 p.m., Sunday from 10:00 a.m.-4:45 p.m.

Pass/Permit/Fees: Adults (18-61): $7, Seniors (62+): $6.50, Youth (6-17): $4.50, Child (under 6): $2

Closest City or Town: Dahlonega, GA

Address: 1 Public Square N, Dahlonega, GA 30533

GPS Coordinates: 34.53376° N, 83.98419° W

Did You Know? With very thorough panning, some people can still find gold deposits in the gravel of the Dahlonega area.

Wolf Mountain Vineyards

Wolf Mountain Vineyards, near Dahlonega, Georgia, is a multi-time winner in several wine competitions. Located in the North Georgia Mountains, Wolf Mountain Vineyards offers beautiful views and amazing wine.

With hillside vineyards, great hospitality and facilities, and amazing views, it is no wonder they have won so many awards over the year. The vineyards are used for hosting wine tastings, weddings, brunch, lunch, or even a fancy dinner.

Best Time to Visit: Open Thursday-Sunday 11-5

Pass/Permit/Fees: No fee to enter; just pay for your beverages or dining

Closest City or Town: Dahlonega, GA

Address: 180 Wolf Mountain Trail, Dahlonega, GA 30533.

GPS Coordinates: 34.59531° N, 83.97639° W

Did You Know? There is not any outdoor seating available, and the brunch/lunch is offered buffet style.

Amicalola Falls

The Amicalola Falls State Park and Lodge cover 829 acres between Ellijay and Dahlonega in Dawsonville, Georgia. The name comes from a Cherokee word that means "tumbling waters."

The highest waterfall in Georgia, with a drop of 729 feet, is found here. Amicalola Falls is considered to be one of the "Seven Natural Wonders of Georgia." Campsites and lodgings are available.

Best Time to Visit: Any time of year

Pass/Permit/Fees: $5 Georgia State Park Pass

Closest City or Town: Dawsonville, GA

Address: Although these falls do not have a specific physical address, you will find them inside Amicalola Falls State Park, located on Amicalola Park Road, Ellijay, GA 30536.

GPS Coordinates: 34.56519° N, 84.23938° W

Did You Know? Hikers and visitors can reach the bottom of the park in 604 steps, with a viewing platform halfway through the journey.

Georgia Guidestones

One of Georgia's most unusual attractions is the Georgia Guidestones, massive granite monuments with guidelines written in twelve different languages. These Guidestones were installed in 1980 and stand as high as 750 feet above sea level.

There is one center stone with four surrounding stones; all astronomically lined up. These Georgia Guidestones are often referred to as the "American Stonehenge" and have often been subject to controversy and various conspiracy theories.

Best Time to Visit: Any time of year

Pass/Permit/Fees: No fee

Closest City or Town: Elberton, GA

Address: 1031 Guidestone Rd. NW, Elberton, GA 30635

GPS Coordinates: 34.23332° N, 82.89444° W

Did You Know? The Georgia Guidestones serve as an astronomical calendar, and every single day as the sun passes around noon, the date is theoretically illuminated on the engraving.

Walter F. George Lake

Walter F. George Lake is an excellent place for people who want to boat, fish, camp and enjoy a picnic lunch. The Chattahoochee River offers great views as well as much to do. The nearby towns of Eufaula, AL, and Cuthbert, GA, are amazing historical sites to discover as well.

This lake, often called Lake Eufaula, is 85 miles long along the Chattahoochee River between Alabama and Georgia. The lake offers 640 miles of shoreline and all of the outdoor activities you can think of!

Best Time to Visit: Any time of year

Pass/Permit/Fees: $5 per vehicle

Closest City or Town: Eufaula, AL

Address: There are multiple access points to Walter F George Reservoir. The ACF/Walter F. George Resource Site is at 427 Eufaula Rd, Fort Gaines, GA 39851.

GPS Coordinates: 31.81251° N, 85.13181° W

Did You Know? Walter F. George Lake is named after Walter F. George, a former U.S. Senator from Georgia.

Robin Lake Beach

Robin Lake Beach is a beautiful white sand beach off Robin Lake, located about one hour from Atlanta and 30 minutes from Columbus. The beach has several amenities, including picnic areas, hiking, and biking trails, a discovery center, butterfly center, bird shows, and more.

There are several seasonal amenities as well, such as boat rentals, souvenir store, snack bar, drink bar, ice cream truck, bikes for rental, and putt-putt mini-golf. Limited beach chairs and umbrellas are also available for rental.

Best Time to Visit: Memorial Day Weekend-Labor Day Weekend, open M-Th 10:00 a.m.-6:00 p.m., F 8:00 a.m.-8 pm, Sat 8:00 a.m.-9:00 p.m., Sun 8:00 a.m.-6:00 p.m.

Pass/Permit/Fees: Visiting the beach is free, but the rentals are all variable costs.

Closest City or Town: Hamilton, GA

Address: There is not a physical address for Robin Lake Beach. However, you can find access to it off of U.S.-27 N on 3 Mile Beach Dr., Pine Mountain, GA.

GPS Coordinates: 32.84601° N, 84.84823° W

Did You Know? Robin Lake Beach is the largest man-made white sand beach in the entire world!

Laurel & Hardy Museum

Laurel and Hardy are two of the most popular comedians of all time, and the Laurel & Hardy Museum is dedicated to honoring and remembering their legacy. The museum is home to several different artifacts, a theater room with a viewing of any of their 106 movies, and so much more.

Hardy was born and raised in Harlem, Georgia, so it should come as no surprise that this is the location for their museum, which thousands of people come to visit every year.

Best Time to Visit: Closed Sundays, open Monday-Saturday from 10:00 a.m.-4:00 p.m.

Pass/Permit/Fees: No fee

Closest City or Town: Harlem, GA

Address: 135 N Louisville St, Harlem, GA 30814.

GPS Coordinates: 33.41520° N, 82.31246° W

Did You Know? The Laurel & Hardy Museum was opened in 2002 and is the only museum in the country that honors these two famously known comedians.

Anna Ruby Falls

Anna Ruby Falls is located near Unicoi State Park and has a large waterfall at the end of a half-mile walk.

The hike, which included a paved trail, is part of the National Recreation Trails in the state of Georgia. Here you can find two waterfalls that are created by the joining of two different streams.

Curtis Creek and York Creek meet at the bottom of the falls and create a pool of water known as Smith Creek. Surrounding the waterfalls is a 1,600-acre scenic area.

Best Time to Visit: Any time of year, 9:00 a.m.-6:00 p.m.

Pass/Permit/Fees: $3 per person

Closest City or Town: Helen, GA

Address: 3455 Anna Ruby Falls Rd, Helen, GA 30545

GPS Coordinates: 34.76536° N, 83.71204° W

Did You Know? Anna Ruby Falls reach heights of 154 feet! The trail is stroller- and dog-friendly and a relatively easy hike slightly uphill. The breathtaking views make it a must-see item when you visit Georgia.

Appalachian Trail

The Appalachian Trail is an excellent place for outdoor enthusiasts to enjoy hiking, running, or climbing through the mountains. The trail stretches 2000+ miles to the north and ends in Maine at Mount Katahdin, passing through 14 states along the way.

In Georgia, there are 78.6 miles of this trail. The southern point is at Springer Mountain. As the trail travels through Georgia, it goes through the Blue Ridge Mountains.

Best Time to Visit: Any time of year

Pass/Permit/Fees: Travelers must make reservations and acquire a permit. People without a permit risk receiving fines up to $125.

Closest City or Town: Helen, GA

Address: There are many access points for the Appalachian Trail throughout Georgia. However, you can access the trail via U.S.-76 E.

GPS Coordinates: 34.91207° N, 83.61864° W

Did You Know? There are several smaller hikes offered in Georgia, including the Appalachian Approach Trail, which is a 15.6-mile round trip hike viewing the Amicalola Falls State Park and Springer Mountain.

Chattahoochee-Oconee National Forest

The Chattahoochee-Oconee National Forest has some of the most enjoyable outdoor recreational things to do in the state.

The forest stretches over 26 counties and covers about 867,000 acres. Here you can find campgrounds, picnic areas, history, and more.

Even if you just stop for a quick picnic lunch, you will enjoy your time visiting the Chattahoochee-Oconee National Forest because it is beautiful and full of breathtaking views. From hiking trails to OHV riding opportunities, this forest has it all.

Best Time to Visit: Any time of the year

Pass/Permit/Fees: If you plan to visit any of the national forests in Georgia, you must first purchase an annual pass for $25.

Closest City or Town: Helen, GA

Address: 48 Forest Service Rd. 44, Helen, GA

GPS Coordinates: 34.76590° N, 84.14398° W

Did You Know? During spring and summer, bears are more likely to be spotted. Always hike with caution when visiting the Chattahoochee-Oconee National Forest.

Dukes Creek Trail

Dukes Creek Trail travels 2.5 miles through a forest full of mountain streams. The trail passes by streams, cascading waterfalls, and the meeting point for Davis and Dukes Creeks. Once you reach the waterfalls, there is a large wooden platform where you can stop and soak in the views of the 150-foot-tall Duke Creek Falls.

The trail offers short length and moderate elevation changes, making it manageable for adults and children alike. If you are interested in breathtaking views of nature, then the Dukes Creek Trail is a must-see attraction for you and your family.

Always be cautious about the slippery rocks along the trail, and do not swim in the water because it is not safe.

Best Time to Visit: Any time of year

Pass/Permit/Fees: $4 per vehicle

Closest City or Town: Helen, GA

Address: 1699 Richard B Russell Scenic Hwy, Helen, GA 30545

GPS Coordinates: 34.70506° N, -83.79020° W

Did You Know? It takes most people about one hour to hike down, soak in the scenery, and hike back.

Helton Creek Falls

Helton Creek Falls features two breathtaking waterfalls on a trail that is less than one mile long. This kid-friendly hike is easily accessible for any age, and it's well worth the effort to witness nature's beauty. Many people would call the hike to the waterfalls a "short walk in the woods."

It is recommended that you pack a picnic lunch to enjoy alongside these beautiful waterfalls because you will want to spend some time enjoying them after you arrive.

The rocks along the trail and in the water are very slippery and dangerous, so be careful not to swim, jump, or climb anywhere near the waterfalls.

Best Time to Visit: Any time of year

Pass/Permit/Fees: No fee

Closest City or Town: Helen, GA

Address: There is not a specific address, but the falls are accessible via the Byron Reece trailhead located at Byron Reece Memorial Trail, Blairsville, GA 30512.

GPS Coordinates: 34.75554° N, 83.89591° W

Did You Know? The vertical drop from Helton Creek Falls is over 100 feet. Because the rocks are slippery, it is not wise to enter the water in this area.

Raven Cliff Falls Trail

The Raven Cliff Falls Trail, 5.8 miles long, includes both a hiking trail and a beautiful view of one of Georgia's waterfalls. There are several things to do around the area, such as camping, hiking, fishing, observing wildlife, and backpacking.

The trail is classified as "moderately strenuous" but also doable for families that have small children. When you complete the hike, you get to enjoy one of the most amazing waterfalls in the eastern part of the United States - the Raven Cliff Falls.

Best Time to Visit: Any time of year, but arrive early because the parking spaces fill up quickly

Pass/Permit/Fees: $5 parking fee

Closest City or Town: Helen, GA

Address: 3000 Richard B Russell Scenic Hwy, Helen, GA 30545

GPS Coordinates: 34.90574° N, 83.86604° W

Did You Know? Raven Cliff Falls is 420 feet high, and the hike is well worth the effort because of the view.

Lake Rabun

Lake Rabun is a reservoir with 25 miles of shoreline in the northeast corner of Georgia. This lake follows the course of the Tallulah River and is used to generate hydroelectric energy for Atlanta.

The dam was created in May of 1915, but the lake was not filled for several years after the completion of the dam. Lake Rabun is the proud sponsor of an antique boat parade and firework display every Fourth of July.

There are several options for boat rentals and lodging, restaurants, wedding venues, and more!

Best Time to Visit: Any time of year

Pass/Permit/Fees: $5 per vehicle per day

Closest City or Town: Hiawassee, GA

Address: 4726 Lake Rabun Rd, Lakemont, GA 30552

GPS Coordinates: 34.76932° N, 83.45931° W

Did You Know? Lake Rabun is home to many dream lake houses along the shoreline.

Driftwood Beach

On the famous Jekyll Island lies the beautiful Driftwood Beach. This is one of the most breathtaking and stunning beaches in the state of Georgia and one worth visiting. The iconic driftwood shores make this beach different from all of the other beaches in the state. The beach is located about five hours from Atlanta, but the beauty of the area makes the drive well worth it for either Instagram or your yearly family photos. Driftwood Beach is a unique area and will be the place where your family makes unforgettable memories.

Best Time to Visit: During the warmer months of the year

Pass/Permit/Fees: No fee

Closest City or Town: Jekyll Island, GA

Address: Parking areas are located off N. Beachview Dr.

From Jekyll Island, head east on Glynn Ave. toward Lanier Rd, turn left onto Lanier Rd. Turn right at the 1st cross street onto Forest Ave, turn left onto Beachview Dr. N/N Loop Trail, and you will arrive at your destination.

GPS Coordinates: 31.11786° N, 81.40960° W

Did You Know? Because of the uniqueness of the area, Driftwood Beach does tend to get pretty crowded in the summer months.

Minnehaha Falls

This easy to moderate hiking trail is 0.4 miles round trip, dog-friendly, and home to one of the most beautiful waterfalls in Georgia: the Minnehaha Falls.

The Minnehaha Falls Trail is very short and easy and well worth the time for the beautiful views. After 0.2 miles, the trail reaches the breathtaking Minnehaha Falls.

While it might be tempting to stick your toes into the water here, it is important to note that the fast-moving water along the slippery rocks is very dangerous.

Standing on rocks, swimming, climbing, and jumping are not allowed at the Minnehaha Falls.

Best Time to Visit: The best time to visit is mid-late May

Pass/Permit/Fees: No fee

Closest City or Town: Lakemont, GA

Address: The Minnehaha Falls Trailhead is located off of Bear Gap Rd., Lakemont, GA 30552.

GPS Coordinates: 34.74753° N, 83.48030° W

Did You Know? The Minnehaha Falls are 100 feet high and cascade down the hill over very large boulders.

Seed Lake

Seed Lake is a great travel destination for the outdoor enthusiast who enjoys discovering nature. At the lake are the Seed Campgrounds, featuring campsites, beaches, picnic areas, restrooms, boat launching ramps, and areas for swimming.

The entire lake covers about 240 acres and is the smallest of the three main reservoirs on the Tallulah River. This lake has only 13 miles of shoreline but a lot of recreational opportunities.

Best Time to Visit: Any time of year

Pass/Permit/Fees: No fee

Closest City or Town: Lakemont, GA

Address: There is not a specific address for this destination, but it is accessed via Bee Blossom Ln., Lakemont, GA 30552.

GPS Coordinates: 34.75589° N, 83.50165° W

Did You Know? Seed Lake was formed in 1927 when the construction of Nacoochee Dam was completed.

Sweetwater Creek State Park

Sweetwater Creek State Park is located very close to Atlanta and is a great place to relax in the wilderness. Here you can find a wooded trail that follows the river to a Civil War manufacturing company that was burned down.

Along the trail, guests can observe the beauty of nature and wildflowers everywhere they look. In the state park lies the George Sparks Reservoir, where people can rent kayaks and boats for fishing or feeding ducks. Picnics are relaxing with beautiful views, but it is not safe to swim in the water here.

Best Time to Visit: Any time of year

Pass/Permit/Fees: $5 per person plus $5 per vehicle for parking; pre-registration is required

Closest City or Town: Lithia Springs, GA

Address: 1750 Mt Vernon Rd., GA 30122

GPS Coordinates: 33.75218° N, 84.62858° W

Did You Know? Sweetwater Creek State Park has two outdoor playgrounds, outdoor exercise equipment, a visitor center, a museum, and a gift shop with wi-fi.

Arabia Mountain

Arabia Mountain is just to the east of Atlanta along I-20 and has several natural wonders that outdoor-loving people must-see. There are two granite outcrops here that include an interesting history as well as breathtaking views.

The Arabia Mountain covers over 40,000 acres of land and has several areas that are perfect for fishing, hiking, or biking. The mountain here is composed of granite, like nearby mountains such as Stone Mountain and Panola Mountain.

Best Time to Visit: Any time of year

Pass/Permit/Fees: No fee for parking or use of trails

Closest City or Town: Lithonia, GA

Address: 3350 Klondike Rd, Stonecrest, GA 30038

GPS Coordinates: 33.66910° N, 84.12013° W

Did You Know? The formation of Arabia Mountain is thought to have begun over 400 million years ago. The peak is 955 feet above sea level!

Providence Canyon State Park

Providence Canyon State Park is considered to be the "Little Grand Canyon" of Georgia, with valleys and gullies as deep as 150 feet.

They were created by bad farming choices back in the 1800s. Fences have been built to protect visitors while allowing them to get a good view of the canyon from the rim trail.

The Park covers 1,003 acres of land and includes several amenities, such as two picnic shelters, three campsites, a museum, and a seasonal visitor center.

Best Time to Visit: Winter

Pass/Permit/Fees: $5 parking pass

Closest City or Town: Lumpkin, GA

Address: 8930 Canyon Rd, Lumpkin, GA 31815

GPS Coordinates: 32.07011° N, 84.91410° W

Did You Know? The Providence Canyon State Park has 16 canyons made by the erosion of soils with varying colors.

Amerson River Park

In Macon, Georgia, lies the Amerson River Park, a 180-acre area full of many aspects of nature to observe. It was originally part of a water treatment plant until a flood swept through the area in 1994. Frank C. Amerson Jr. then decided to transform the destroyed area into a park to serve the community. From forests and meadows to wetlands and a river, there is much outdoor nature to enjoy and explore. The park features a handicap-accessible playground, over seven miles of walking and running trails, and the nearby Ocmulgee River.

Many people use the river for various recreational activities such as kayaking, canoeing, floating on a tube, and more. If you decide to float the river park, expect it to take roughly two hours.

Best Time to Visit: Open daily from 7:30 a.m.-8:00 p.m.

Pass/Permit/Fees: No fee

Closest City or Town: Macon, GA

Address: 2551 Pierce Dr. N, Macon, GA 31204.

GPS Coordinates: 32.87466° N, 83.65582° W

Did You Know? Amerson River Park stretches for 1.8 miles.

Johnston-Felton-Hay House

The Johnston-Felton-Hay-House, more commonly known as the Hay House, is a historical house from 1855-1859. This area, nicknamed the "palace of the south," is on top of a giant hill near the Walter F. George School of Law. In 1973, this beautiful home was designated as a National Historic Landmark.

The Hay House contains 18,000 square feet and 24 rooms built in the craftsman style. It is four levels high and well worth a visit. The house has been turned into a private house museum where guests can see what architecture and everyday life were like during the 1800s.

Best Time to Visit: Any time of year, open every day from 10:00 a.m.-4:00 p.m., closed on Monday and Tuesday

Pass/Permit/Fees: $4 per person for the house tour

Closest City or Town: Macon, GA

Address: 934 Georgia Ave, Macon, GA 31201

GPS Coordinates: 32.84110° N, 83.63120° W

Did You Know? The house has beautiful marble statues, stunning stained glass, and original period decorations and paintings.

Ocmulgee Mounds National Historical Park

The Ocmulgee Mounds National Historical Park includes various nature sites, such as the Great Temple, ceremonial and burial mounds, and trenches used in warfare. The park is home to 702 acres of land with 5.5 miles of walking trails.

The historical park has a visitor center featuring other surviving structures that have been excavated by archeologists. In 1100 AD, the park was completely abandoned, and it is not known what happened to the people who lived here.

The area became a national park in 1936 under President Franklin D. Roosevelt.

Best Time to Visit: Open daily from 8:00 a.m.-5:00 p.m.

Pass/Permit/Fees: No fee

Closest City or Town: Macon, GA

Address: 1207 Emery Hwy, Macon, GA 31217.

GPS Coordinates: 32.84896° N, 83.59986° W

Did You Know? The Great Temple Mound was used for various religious ceremonies and was 50 feet tall.

Tattnall Square Park

The Tattnall Square Park in Macon, Georgia, is a great place to take your dog for a walk or your children to play on the playgrounds. With a dog park in the area, it is a safe space to allow your pet to run and burn energy while staying in an enclosed area away from vehicles.

The park frequently hosts outdoor movie screenings and special events such as festivals, and it's a great picnic location. The park is the second oldest park in the state of Georgia and one of the oldest parks in the entire country.

Best Time to Visit: Open Sunday 1-6:00 p.m., Monday-Thursday 8:30am-9:00 p.m., Friday 8:30am-7:30pm, Saturday 8:00 a.m.-2:30pm

Pass/Permit/Fees: No fee

Closest City or Town: Macon, GA

Address: 1155 College St, Macon, GA 31201.

GPS Coordinates: 32.83422° N, 83.64627° W

Did You Know? Union troops set up camp at Tattnall Square Park during their occupation of Georgia in the Civil War.

The Allman Brothers Band Museum

The Allman Brothers Band Museum, commonly called "the Big House," is in Macon, Georgia. It was the home of the Allman Brothers Band members from 1970-1973. The house was also a common place of residence for their families and friends as well.

In 2009, the house was renovated and reopened to the public to create an interactive museum to honor and remember the band's legacy. Guests are welcome to visit and learn more about the Allman Brothers Band at their personal museum.

Best Time to Visit: Open Sunday 11:00 a.m.-4:00 p.m., closed Monday-Wednesday, Open Thursday-Saturday 11:00 a.m.-6:00 p.m.

Pass/Permit/Fees: Children 10-18: $10, Seniors: $13, Adult: $15

Closest City or Town: Macon, GA

Address: 2321 Vineville Ave, Macon, GA, 31204.

GPS Coordinates: 32.84686° N, 83.65422° W

Did You Know? The proud owners of The Big House are Kirk and Kristen West, two people who have worked very hard to honor the band's legacy and create a space to remember The Allman Brothers Band.

92

The Cannonball House

The Cannonball House, built in 1853, earned its name in 1864 when a cannonball fired by the Union Army during the Civil War struck one of its columns, passed through the parlor, and came to rest in an inside hallway.

This beautiful Greek Revival home is listed in the National Register of Historic Places. A bronze cannon displayed on the front lawn was forged in 1864 at the Macon Arsenal.

The house holds a collection of Civil War artifacts and a gift shop. Visitors can also explore the garden and join historical and educational tours.

Best Time to Visit: Closed Sundays, Open Monday-Saturday 10:00 a.m.-3:30 p.m.

Pass/Permit/Fees: Adult $8, Students $4, under 4 free

Closest City or Town: Macon, GA

Address: 856 Mulberry St, Macon, GA 31201.

GPS Coordinates: 32.84097° N, 83.63133° W

Did You Know? Most things that get hit with a cannonball are destroyed, but this house survived and was marked as a historical landmark because of it.

Tubman Museum

The Tubman Museum, formerly known as the Tubman African American Museum, was founded in 1981 in a period-original home and moved to its present location in 2015. The museum features displays and exhibits focused on African American history and culture.

Located in the museum district of Macon, Georgia, it contains 8,500 square feet full of rich history and art from the past. The purpose of the Tubman Museum is to educate the public on African American history and culture through programs, exhibits, and classes.

Best Time to Visit: Closed Sunday-Monday, Open Tuesday-Saturday 9:00 a.m.-5:00 p.m.

Pass/Permit/Fees: Adult: $10, Children: $6

Closest City or Town: Macon, GA

Address: 310 Cherry St, Macon, GA, 31201.

GPS Coordinates: 32.83440° N, 83.62317° W

Did You Know? The Tubman Museum is the largest in the country dedicated to educating the public on African American history and culture.

Warm Springs

The small city of Warm Springs is about one hour south of Atlanta and is home to exactly what you would think – warm springs! These naturally heated areas of mineral water were made famous by Franklin D. Roosevelt and offer a lot of history to discover and enjoy while visiting Georgia.

Here guests can find restored 100+-year-old buildings, shopping, dining, museums, and much southern charm. The Warm Springs area is always hosting a festival or innovative program. Be sure to check the schedule before your visit, so you do not miss a thing!

Best Time to Visit: Any time of year

Pass/Permit/Fees: No fee to visit

Closest City or Town: Manchester, GA

Address: 1 Broad St, Warm Springs, GA 31830

GPS Coordinates: 32.88752° N, 84.67455° W

Did You Know? One thing that makes Warm Springs famous is the Little White House, the place where Roosevelt vacationed and died in 1945. This location is now a public museum full of so much rich history.

Springer Mountain

Springer Mountain is one of the state's most popular and highly visited hiking locations because of the beautiful views of the Blue Ridge Mountains. The Appalachian Trail (AT) takes off from the summit of Springer Mountain, as do the Benton MacKaye Trail (BMT) and several other hiking trails. There are a few different options to get the best views; the first is a 2-mile hike from Springer Mountain to the mountain's summit.

A slightly longer hike is the Springer Mountain Loop on the AT and BMT, which loops around the mountain for a duration of 5.1 miles. The longest and most difficult option is the 8.6-mile hike known as Three Forks to Springer Mountain.

Best Time to Visit: The best time to visit is in the fall when the temperatures are cooler and the leaves are changing.

Pass/Permit/Fees: No fee

Closest City or Town: Nimblewill, GA

Address: Forest Service Road 42, Blue Ridge, GA 30513

GPS Coordinates: 34.63989° N, 84.19428° W

Did You Know? The peak of Springer Mountain is 3,780 feet above sea level!

Callaway Gardens

Callaway Gardens is a great family resort destination for several different reasons. From seasonal hot air balloon festivals to golf courses on site, there is something for everyone.

The Callaway Gardens resort also has a beach for guests to enjoy and gardens to explore. Callaway Gardens is home to botanical gardens that allow guests to enjoy a ton of plant life and learn more about the flowers that grow in this area. With hiking and bike trails, there is much to explore at the Callaway Gardens.

Best Time to Visit: Any time of year, open from 9:00 a.m.-dusk

Pass/Permit/Fees: Adult: $29.95, Child: $19.95

Closest City or Town: Pine Mountain, GA

Address: 17800 U.S. Hwy 27, Pine Mountain, GA 31822

GPS Coordinates: 32.83070° N, 84.84271° W

Did You Know? While one might think the Callaway Gardens are most famous for their beautiful flowers, they are equally as famous for their world-class golf courses.

Jimmy Carter National Historic Site

The Jimmy Carter National Historic Site is a set of locations that have been preserved to honor and remember the country's 39th President, James Earl "Jimmy" Carter Jr. The sites include his childhood home, farm, school, and a railroad depot that was the campaign headquarters for the election in 1976.

The former school which Jimmy Carter and his wife attended is now the visitor center and museum for the historic site. Inside are a classroom, principal's office, and auditorium. Guests are welcome to explore the area and see what life was like in the 1920s when Carter was a young boy.

Best Time to Visit: Any time of year, open daily from 9:00 a.m.-5:00 p.m.

Pass/Permit/Fees: No fee

Closest City or Town: Plains, GA

Address: 300 N Bond St, Plains, GA 31780.

GPS Coordinates: 32.03679° N, 84.39257° W

Did You Know? Jimmy Carter was the first United States President who was born and raised in Georgia.

National Museum of the Mighty Eighth Air Force

This museum is in Pooler, Georgia, very close to Savannah. It uses exhibits, stories, and artifacts to educate the public about the Eighth Air Force from the USAF during World War II. A B-17 Flying Fortress bomber and models of WWII fighters. Several jet fighters are displayed outside the museum. The National Museum of the Mighty Eighth Air Force also has an art gallery, restaurant, gift shop, and memorial garden.

Planning for the museum began in 1983, and it opened in May 1996.

Best Time to Visit: Open Sundays noon-5:00 p.m., closed Mondays, Open Tuesday-Saturday 10:00 a.m.-5:00 p.m.

Pass/Permit/Fees: Adult $12, Child $8, Senior/Military/Students $11

Closest City or Town: Pooler, GA

Address: 175 Bourne Ave, Pooler, GA, 31322

GPS Coordinates: 32.11597° N, 81.23390° W

Did You Know? The museum has a "mission experience" that allows guests to experience what it was like during a bombing mission.

Cloudland Canyon State Park

Cloudland Canyon, on the western side of Lookout Mountain, is one of the largest parks in the state. The park contains several thousand-foot-deep canyons, cliffs, caves, waterfalls, and creeks.

Hiking and biking trails are available, including the short Overlook Trail, Waterfall Trail, and the West Rim Loop Trail. The park also has disc golf, picnic tables, and camping sites.

Best Time to Visit: Any time of year

Pass/Permit/Fees: $5 per day for 1-12 passenger vehicles or $50 annual Park Pass. $30 per day for 13-30 passenger vehicles or $75 Park Pass. $70 per day for 31+ passenger vehicles or $250 annual Park Pass. For active-duty military/veterans, $3.75 per day or $37.50 annual Park Pass.

Closest City or Town: Rising Fawn, GA

Address: 122 Cloudland Canyon Park Rd, Rising Fawn, GA 30738.

GPS Coordinates: 34.83873° N, 85.48323° W

Did You Know? The Civilian Conservation Corps did much of the work to construct the park, beginning in 1939.

Lookout Mountain

Lookout Mountain, Georgia, is right on the border of Lookout Mountain, Tennessee, just 6 miles away. The entire area covers about 2.7 square miles and is home to the popular Rock City.

Rock City and Lookout Mountain have amazing ancient rock structures, gardens with more than 400 plants, and panoramic views. The mountain hosts some holiday events and has several bed and breakfast locations for guests to enjoy.

Best Time to Visit: Any time of year

Pass/Permit/Fees: For event admission, adults are $26.95, and children (ages 3-12) are $14.95.

Closest City or Town: Rising Fawn, GA

Address: To reach the top of Lookout Mountain, take the Scenic Highway by car or the Lookout Mountain Incline Railway at 3917 St Elmo Ave, Chattanooga, TN 37409.

GPS Coordinates: 34.86664° N, 85.39319° W

Did You Know? Lookout Mountain runs from Birmingham to Knoxville and reaches an elevation of 2,393 feet.

Nanny Goat Beach

Nanny Goat Beach is along the southeastern side of Sapelo Island and must be reached via ferry.

The Georgia Department of Natural Resources offers a short ferry ride for guests to get to the island safely. The only other way to reach the island is by aircraft.

At Nanny Goat Beach are picnic tables, toilets, sheltered pavilions facing the ocean, beautiful beaches with white sand, and amazing wildlife and plant life.

Best Time to Visit: Any time of year

Pass/Permit/Fees: $5 per person for a ferry ride

Closest City or Town: Sapelo Island, GA

Address: To catch a ferry ride, start your trip at the Sapelo Island Visitors Center located at 1766 Landing Rd, Darien, GA 31305.

GPS Coordinates: 31.39828° N, 81.25626° W

Did You Know? Nanny Goat Beach is located close to the Gray's Reef National Marine Sanctuary, the largest live-bottom reef in the Southeast.

Bull Street

Bull Street is a very rich area for historical discovery and exploration. There are streets lined with granite curbs, sidewalks made of bricks, and beautiful landscaping to make the area stunning and worth visiting.

Several restaurants, shops, and boutiques are located in the Bull Street area. There's also the Savannah Theatre, where shows are available for adults at the cost of $35 and children (17 and under) for $17.

Bookstores, amazing cupcakes, and more are also available on the famous Bull Street.

Best Time to Visit: Any time of year

Pass/Permit/Fees: No fee

Closest City or Town: Savannah, GA

Address: There is not a specific address, but Bull Street is accessed from Bay St.

GPS Coordinates: 33.44256° N, 82.11026° W

Did You Know? Bull Street is named after Colonel William Bull and runs for 3.4 miles through Savannah, Georgia.

Cathedral of St. John the Baptist

The Cathedral of St. John the Baptist was started right before the end of the 18th century when the congregation came to the United States from Haiti. After years of struggle trying to get the building erected and the congregation grown, the church was rebuilt in 1835.

Guests are welcome to visit the Cathedral of St. John the Baptist. Several events are hosted in the Cathedral Basilica of St. John the Baptist. If you want to watch mass, it is live-streamed on their website during Covid-19 times.

Best Time to Visit: If you are visiting for mass, the church meets every Sunday at 10. To visit the cathedral, come any time other than the scheduled mass.

Pass/Permit/Fees: No fee

Closest City or Town: Savannah, GA

Address: 222 E Harris St., Savannah, GA 31401

GPS Coordinates: 32.07359° N, 81.08992° W

Did You Know? The pointed arches and French-Gothic style of the Cathedral of St. John the Baptist are beautiful against the Savannah skyline.

Forsyth Park

In the heart of Savannah, GA, lies the beautiful Forsyth Park, a 30-acre park that was named after the 33rd governor of Georgia. The center point of the park is the fountain that was installed in 1858 and is reminiscent of the fountains at the Place de la Concorde in Paris. This beautiful fountain is the location of numerous proposals, weddings, and other events.

Inside the park are two children's playgrounds, one for younger children and one for older. The park has a concert area, a splash pad, and a beautiful garden. The giant green fields in Forsyth Park are great napping, lounging, and relaxing areas for guests, with a to-go juice bar, coffee shop, and a Saturday Farmer's Market. The park holds several festivals and concerts throughout the year and is very popular with both locals and tourists.

Best Time to Visit: Any time of year

Pass/Permit/Fees: No fee

Closest City or Town: Savannah, GA

Address: 2 W Gaston St, Savannah, GA 31401.

GPS Coordinates: 32.06873° N, 81.09550° W

Did You Know? The fountain in the middle of the park is over 150 years old!

Fort McAllister State Historic Park

Fort McAllister State Historic Park in Richmond Hill, Georgia, covers 1,725 acres of land. This park is located right along the banks of the Ogeechee River and is a quick ten miles away from Savannah.

During the Civil War, this area was attacked unsuccessfully seven times but held strong until it was taken in 1864. The park is surrounded by beautiful oak trees and a salt marsh nearby. There is also a museum that houses several Civil War artifacts.

Best Time to Visit: Any time of year

Pass/Permit/Fees: 1-12 passenger vehicles $5 per day or $50 annual Park Pass; 13-30 passenger vehicles $30 per day or $75 annual Park Pass.

Closest City or Town: Savannah, GA

Address: 3894 Fort McAllister Rd, Richmond Hill, GA 31324.

GPS Coordinates: 31.89172° N, 81.19569° W

Did You Know? Fort McAllister was a key location and one of the most important ports for the Confederates along the Atlantic Ocean.

Golden Isles

The Golden Isles encompasses four beautiful islands: St. Simons Island, Sea Island, Jekyll Island, and Little St. Simons Island, and the mainland port city of Brunswick. These beautiful stretches of marshland appear as one giant stretch of land to the barrier islands.

Best Time to Visit: Many people find spring and fall to be very enjoyable times to visit the Golden Isles.

Pass/Permit/Fees: $8 for one car per day or $55 for a 12-month parking pass. For oversized vehicles, the cost is slightly higher at $12 per day and $100 for a year pass.

Closest City or Town: Savannah, GA

Address: The Golden Isles Welcome Center is located at 529 Beachview Dr., St Simons Island, GA 31522, which offers local information.

GPS Coordinates: 31.13668° N, 81.39505° W

Did You Know? The islands got their name from the coast's earliest explorers, who searched for glittering treasures and other riches.

Juliette Gordon Low Historic District

This district contains three buildings: the Juliette Gordon Low Birthplace, the First Girl Scout Headquarters, which was the carriage house for the Andrew Low House, and the Andrew Low House itself.

In 1911, Juliette Gordon Low met Robert Baden Powell, founder of the Boy Scouts, who got her involved with the Girl Guides. She returned home to Savannah in 1912 and founded the Girl Scouts of America (GSA). The GSA bought the home in 1953 and restored it to serve as a portal to the Girl Scout Movement.

Best time to visit: Open from 10:00 a.m.-4:00 p.m. Mon.-Tue. and Thu.-Sat.

Pass/Permit/Fees: $10 for registered Girl Scouts, $15 Adults, $12 Seniors/Military

Closest City or Town: Savannah, GA

Address: 10 E Oglethorpe Ave, Savannah, GA 31401

GPS Coordinates: 32.07725° N, 81.09241° W

Did You Know? The store at Juliette Gordon Low Birthplace likes to focus on women-owned businesses and sells many items made by girls and women from around the country.

Old Fort Jackson

Old Fort Jackson is a restored fort one mile east of Savannah. At this location is the Fort Jackson Maritime Museum, all honoring and remembering James Jackson, who served as an officer in the American Revolution and later became a U.S. representative and senator.

The fort was built between1808 and 1812 to protect the city from attack by sea, and it was one of three forts that protected Savannah during the Civil War.

If you visit the fort during the summertime, you will more than likely get a demonstration of an actual cannon being fired.

Best Time to Visit: Open daily from 9:00 a.m.-4:00 p.m.

Pass/Permit/Fees: $7 for adults, $4 for children, daily cannon firing is at 10:00 a.m. during the Spring and Summer months

Closest City or Town: Savannah, GA

Address: 1 Fort Jackson Rd, Savannah, GA 31404.

GPS Coordinates: 32.08244° N, 81.03387° W

Did You Know? The Old Fort Jackson is the oldest standing brick fort in Georgia.

Owens-Thomas House

The Owens-Thomas House is one of many historic houses in Savannah that has since been turned into a museum full of artifacts and time original pieces. Built from 1816 to 1819, the house was named a National Historic Landmark in 1976 as a fine example of English Regency architecture.

During the 1990s, renovations were done on the house, and the urban slave quarters were discovered. The restoration included the pantry and the cellar where meals and laundry were done.

The Owens-Thomas House features a museum with decorative pieces that belonged to the Owens family as well as pieces from the slave quarters.

Best Time to Visit: Open every day except Wednesdays from 10:00 a.m.-5:00 p.m.

Pass/Permit/Fees:

Closest City or Town: Savannah, GA

Address: 124 Abercorn St, Savannah, GA 31401

GPS Coordinates: 32.07832° N, 81.08911° W

Did You Know? Anywhere from 9 to 15 slaves worked at this site from the early 1800s until the end of the Civil War in 1865.

Ralph Mark Gilbert Civil Rights Museum

In Savannah, Georgia, the Ralph Mark Gilbert Civil Rights Museum lays out the history of African American culture from the time of slavery until the present day. The main focus of this museum is on the civil rights movement.

The Reverend Dr. Ralph Mark Gilbert played a crucial role in the civil rights movement. The museum named for him was created to archive his sermons, which were written and presented in Savannah. Here at the museum are several floors of exhibits that allow guests to learn more about this rich history while having an interactive experience doing so.

Best Time to Visit: Any time of year

Pass/Permit/Fees: $10 for adults, $6 for students,

Closest City or Town: Savannah, GA

Address: 460 Martin Luther King Jr Blvd, Savannah, GA, 31401.

GPS Coordinates: 32.07348° N, 81.09794° W

Did You Know? The Ralph Mark Gilbert Civil Rights Museum is always looking for more artifacts to add to its collection and is open to taking items if guests happen to have any items related to the civil rights movement.

Savannah Historic District

Downtown Savannah is home to the famous Historic District, where guests can find different landmarks on every single corner of the area. There are 22 park squares, monuments, restored homes, boutiques, over 100 restaurants, and so much to explore and do in this small area.

Some less common activities are available, such as a ghost tour or a ferry ride down the Savannah River, allowing visitors to soak in the beauty of the history and the town. An old trolley takes guests on a ride through the old town, something that is memorable for all ages.

Best Time to Visit: The best time to visit is between March and July, when the azaleas are in full bloom.

Pass/Permit/Fees: No fee for walking the district

Closest City or Town: Savannah, GA

Address: 301 Martin Luther King Jr Blvd, Savannah, GA 31401

GPS Coordinates: 32.07816° N, 81.09799° W

Did You Know? The town of Savannah was a Christmas gift given to President Lincoln during the Civil War.

Squares of Savannah

The Squares of Savannah are the most loved parts of the city, offering parks and iconic views at each spot. When the Squares of Savannah were originally planned out, there were 24 different squares, but only 22 of them are left today.

The Squares of Savannah are Calhoun Square, Chatham Square, Chippewa Square, Columbus Square, Crawford Square, Elbert Square, Ellis Square, Franklin Square, Greene Square, Johnson Square, Lafayette Square, Liberty Square, Madison Square, Monterey Square, Oglethorpe Square, Orleans Square, Pulaski Square, Reynolds Square, Telfair Square, Troup Square, Warren Square, Washington Square, Whitefield Square, and Wright Square.

Best Time to Visit: Any time of year

Pass/Permit/Fees: No fee

Closest City or Town: Savannah, GA

Address: 127 Abercorn St, Savannah, GA 31401.

GPS Coordinates: 32.07847° N, 81.09027° W

Did You Know? The few squares that are no longer in existence were destroyed by urban sprawl in the 1900s.

Telfair Academy of Arts and Sciences

The Telfair Academy of Arts and Sciences became an art museum open to the public free of charge in 1886. It was one of the very first art museums in the country. The original building was designed by William Jay and built in 1818 as the Telfair family's townhouse.

Telfair Academy of Arts and Sciences has a wide variety of artifacts, including fully furnished rooms with original pieces and decor. Outside the building are several statues by Rembrandt, Phidias, Rubens, Raphael, and Michelangelo. The subjects include emperors, philosophers, mythological creatures, military heroes, and more.

Best Time to Visit: Open daily from 10:00 a.m.-5:00 p.m., closed on Wednesdays

Pass/Permit/Fees: No fee

Closest City or Town: Savannah, GA

Address: 121 Barnard St, Savannah, GA, 31401.

GPS Coordinates: 32.07984° N, 81.09359° W

Did You Know? The mansion housing the Telfair Academy of Arts and Sciences was once known as "The Little Place." It is rumored that a ghost stalks the mansion, bitter about an unrequited love affair!

Tybee Island

People have been visiting Tybee Island since the late 1800s for many different reasons, including the historical landmarks and the beautiful outdoor views. There are fishing areas, children's playgrounds, and multiple beaches to enjoy.

Weather is excellent year-round at Tybee Island, usually between the mid-70s and low-90s. There are many different restaurants and shops as well as a science center and things to do for the entire family.

Best Time to Visit: Any time of year

Pass/Permit/Fees: $3.50 per hour for parking

Closest City or Town: Savannah, GA

Address: Tybee Island is accessed via Old U.S. Hwy 80. There are many things to see, but to start your adventure, the Tybee Island Light Station & Museum is found at 30 Meddin Dr., Tybee Island, GA 31328

GPS Coordinates: 32.00924° N, 80.84404° W

Did You Know? From May 1 until October 31, endangered sea turtles come to Tybee Island to lay eggs.

Wormsloe Historic Site

Often called Wormsloe Plantation, this site in Savannah covers 822 acres. The estate was founded in 1736 by Noble Jones, a Georgia colonial founder. Given to the Wormsloe family by George II of England, the plantation originally forced slaves to carve out the original 500 acres of land, which continued until the Civil War.

One of George's oldest tidewater estates, most of the site was acquired by the state in 1973 was opened to the public in 1979. The site includes 1.5 miles of oak-lined avenue, the remains of Jones' home, a museum, and an area where demonstrations show what life was once like in this area.

Best Time to Visit: Open daily from 9:00 a.m.-4:45 p.m.

Pass/Permit/Fees:

Closest City or Town: Savannah, GA

Address: 7601 Skidaway Rd, Savannah, GA 31406.

GPS Coordinates: 31.98099° N, 81.06744° W

Did You Know? During the Civil War, the Wormsloe Plantation was taken by Union forces in 1864, and the family was forced to flee the area.

Cumberland Island

Just off the southeastern shore of Georgia lies Cumberland Island, a wonderful place for exploring protected beaches. The island was inhabited by its natural owners for 4,000 years before the Spanish occupation in the 1550s. The Mocama missionaries created a garrison and mission named San Pedro de Mocama. The English did not arrive until 1733. In the 1742 Battle of Bloody Marsh, the Spanish were defeated. There are many ruins, much history, and loggerhead turtles and feral horses roam the island. When visiting Cumberland Island, most people choose to travel around on a bike because cars are not permitted

Best Time to Visit: Camping is best in December, January, or February when the weather is ideal and bugs are fewer.

Pass/Permit/Fees: Guests must pay a ferry fee to reach the island but, to enter the park, adults (16+) must pay $10 for one week; children (15 and under) are free.

Closest City or Town: St. Marys, GA

Address: 113 St. Marys St, St. Marys, GA 31558.

GPS Coordinates: 30.86953° N, 81.43793° W

Did You Know? French pirates attacked the island in 1683, and the island was attacked again in 1684 by a Spanish pirate known as Thomas Jingle.

Sea Island Golf Course

There isn't anything much more relaxing than a nice game of golf played on the seaside, and that is why Sea Island Golf Course exists! The course itself is challenging and exciting for golfers to soak in the views and enjoy the game.

A distinctive feature of the Sea Island Golf Course is that there is almost always a fresh breeze blowing through the area. This particular golf course is rated as one of the top 100 courses in the entire country, and for good reason. With beautiful greens and fairways, the Sea Island Golf Course is a must-play course for golf fanatics.

Best Time to Visit: Open daily from 7:00 a.m.-6:00 p.m.

Pass/Permit/Fees: Seaside Course 18 holes: $250, 9 holes (after 4:00 p.m.) and replay rate - $150

Closest City or Town: St. Simons Island, GA

Address: 100 Retreat Ave, St. Simons Island, GA 31522.

GPS Coordinates: 31.14319° N, 81.40639° W

Did You Know? The PGA Tour's RSM Classic is held at Sea Island every year.

Bridal Veil Falls

The Bridal Veil Falls experience takes hikers as close to a waterfall as they wish, while most of the trail takes you on the northern side of the river. No actual trail is mapped out, so the hiker must decide which path to take in several different situations.

Starting at the visitors' center, this hike goes directly to Bridal Veil Falls, where you can play in the water and even slide down the falls. A rope is in the water so you can pull yourself out of the river if necessary. Snakes have been reported in this area, so if you get in the water, be sure to stay as safe as possible.

Best Time to Visit: Any time of year

Pass/Permit/Fees: There is a parking fee of $5 per car to enter the park.

Closest City or Town: Tallulah Falls, GA

Address: There is no specific physical address for Bridal Veil Falls, but it starts at the visitors' center off Hwy 441 in Tallulah Falls, GA 30573.

GPS Coordinates: 34.73566° N, 83.38504° W

Did You Know? The Bridal Veil Falls is 617 feet high!

Tallulah Gorge

Tallulah Gorge is a stunning canyon in the eastern part of the state that includes a 2-mile hike going 1,000 feet deep into the canyon. Guests are allowed to walk across a suspension bridge that towers 80 feet above the gorge, offering amazing views of the water and waterfalls below.

A more advanced trail for mountain bikers, strollers, etc., follows an old railroad bed for 10 miles. The Tallulah Gorge covers 2,739 acres of land, including a 63-acre lake. Due to limited space, be sure to check in before your arrival and make sure you have a reservation.

Best Time to Visit: The best time to visit is between March and June or September to November.

Pass/Permit/Fees: $5 entrance fee

Closest City or Town: Tallulah Falls, GA

Address: 338 Jane Hurt Yarn Rd., Tallulah Falls, GA 30573

GPS Coordinates: 34.74458° N, 83.39044° W

Did You Know? The word "Tallulah" means "loud waters" in Cherokee, which should come as no surprise because there are several waterfalls in the area.

Toccoa Falls

Toccoa Falls is on the campus of Toccoa Falls College in Stephens County, Georgia. The Cherokee word "toccoa" means "beautiful."

This stunning waterfall features a drop of 186 feet, 26 feet higher than Niagara Falls, which makes it the highest single-drop waterfall on the eastern side of the Mississippi River.

A gift shop located at the falls and the entire waterfall is handicapped-accessible.

Best Time to Visit: Any time of year from 8:30 a.m. until sundown

Pass/Permit/Fees: Adults: $2, Children: $1

Closest City or Town: Toccoa, GA

Address: 107 Kincaid Dr., Toccoa Falls, GA 30598

GPS Coordinates: 34.59747° N, 83.35997° W

Did You Know? On November 6, 1977, a tragic event happened when the dam broke and killed 39 people in this area.

Panther Creek Falls

One of the most popular hikes in Georgia is at Panther Creek Falls, where a 7-mile hike takes you to the beautiful waterfall. It's made up of a series of several tiers that fall into a pool with a beach below. Many people enjoy soaking up the sun and beauty in the sandy flat beneath the falls.

The trail to the waterfall is studded with campsites. Visitors are warned not to climb, stand on, swim near, or jump from any waterfall because the slippery rocks and fast-moving water can be extremely dangerous!

Best Time to Visit: The best time to visit is anywhere from March to October.

Pass/Permit/Fees: Parking costs $4

Closest City or Town: Turnerville, GA

Address: The falls are only accessible via the Panther Creek Trail located at 4061 Old Historic U.S. 441, Clarkesville, GA.

GPS Coordinates: 34.67853° N, 83.39208° W

Did You Know? As of October 2020, the trail had severe storm damage, and two bridges were completely ruined. Due to this sad situation, the trail has been temporarily closed.

Rock City Gardens

Rock City Gardens, atop Lookout Mountain, features massive rock formations from ancient times. This area has over 400 native plant species and breathtaking panoramic views.

The Enchanted Trail allows guests to see the true beauty of the state and includes a gift shop offering souvenirs. There are several restaurant and shopping opportunities as well as a venue for weddings and other large gatherings.

Best Time to Visit: The best time to visit is during the fall, from September to November.

Pass/Permit/Fees: Adult: $21.95, Children: $12.95, Under 3: Free

Closest City or Town: West Brow, GA

Address: 1400 Patten Rd, Lookout Mountain, GA 30750

GPS Coordinates: 34.97349° N, 85.34987° W

Did You Know? Rock City Gardens offers several seasonal events, including an Irish festival in March, a corn maze in the valley below the gardens in autumn, and an "Enchanted Garden of Lights" in November and December.

Allatoona Lake

This lake covers over 12,000 acres and has about 270 miles of shore to explore and enjoy. The lake and surrounding areas are maintained by the U.S. Army Corps of Engineers.

A lot of the land surrounding the lake is rented out for private events, but there are public areas with facilities, as well. Eight marinas offer services ranging from boat sales and rentals to storage options. You can also find many restaurants, camping areas, cabins, and other useful facilities.

Best Time to Visit: Any time of year

Pass/Permit/Fees: $5 parking, $5 boat launching fee. An annual day pass can be purchased for $40

Closest City or Town: Woodstock, GA

Address: There is not a specific physical address for Allatoona Lake. You can gain access via Victoria Park Beach, which is located in Woodstock, GA.

GPS Coordinates: 34.15397° N, 84.61977° W

Did You Know? The lake was created from the construction of the Etowah River dam in 1949 for flood control, hydroelectric power, and wildlife preservation.

Proper Planning

With this guide, you are well on your way to properly planning a marvelous adventure. When you plan your travels, you should become familiar with the area, save any maps to your phone for access without internet, and bring plenty of water—especially during the summer months. Depending on which adventure you choose, you will also want to bring snacks or even a lunch. For younger children, you should do your research and find destinations that best suit your family's needs. You should also plan when and where to get gas, local lodgings, and food. We've done our best to group these destinations based on nearby towns and cities to help make planning easier.

Dangerous Wildlife

There are several dangerous animals and insects you may encounter while hiking. With a good dose of caution and awareness, you can explore safely. Here are steps you can take to keep yourself and your loved ones safe from dangerous flora and fauna while exploring:

- Keep to the established trails.
- Do not look under rocks, leaves, or sticks.
- Keep hands and feet out of small crawl spaces, bushes, covered areas, or crevices.
- Wear long sleeves and pants to keep arms and legs protected.
- Keep your distance should you encounter any dangerous wildlife or plants.

Limited Cell Service

Do not rely on cell service for navigation or emergencies. Always have a map with you and let someone know where you are and how long you intend to be gone, just in case.

First Aid Information

Always travel with a first aid kit in case of emergencies.

Here are items you should be certain to include in your primary first aid kit:

- Nitrile gloves
- Blister care products
- Band-Aids in multiple sizes and waterproof type
- Ace wrap and athletic tape
- Alcohol wipes and antibiotic ointment
- Irrigation syringe
- Tweezers, nail clippers, trauma shears, safety pins
- Small zip-lock bags containing contaminated trash

It is recommended to also keep a secondary first aid kit, especially when hiking, for more serious injuries or medical emergencies. Items in this should include:

- Blood clotting sponges
- Sterile gauze pads
- Trauma pads
- Second-skin/burn treatment
- Triangular bandages/sling
- Butterfly strips
- Tincture of benzoin

- Medications (ibuprofen, acetaminophen, antihistamine, aspirin, etc.)
- Thermometer
- CPR mask
- Wilderness medicine handbook
- Antivenin

There is much more to explore, but this is a great start.

For information on all national parks, visit https://www.nps.gov/index.htm .

This site will give you information on up-to-date entrance fees and how to purchase a park pass for unlimited access to national and state parks. This site will also introduce you to all of the trails at each park.

Always check before you travel to destinations to make sure there are no closures. Some hiking trails close when there is heavy rain or snow in the area and other parks close parts of their land for the migration of wildlife. Attractions may change their hours or temporarily shut down for various reasons. Check the websites for the most up-to-date information.

Made in the USA
Las Vegas, NV
07 December 2022

61183256R00079